I0754799

PARVA **Convivia** III

PLOTINUS·AND·THE·ORIGINS OF·MEDIEVAL·AESTHETICS

ANDRÉ GRABAR

PLOTINUS·AND THE·ORIGINS OF·MEDIEVAL AESTHETICS

TRANSLATION, INTRODUCTION & EDITING ■ ADRIEN PALLADINO

Masaryk University, Brno & Viella, Rome
2018

This book, introduction and translation of the text were carried out as parts of the ongoing project "The Heritage of Nikodim Pavlovič Kondakov in the Experiences of André Grabar and the Seminarium Kondakovianum" (Czech Science Foundation, Reg. № 18-20666s).

ORIGINAL TITLE • André Grabar, *Plotin et les origines de l'esthétique médiévale*

TRANSLATION • Adrien Palladino

TYPESETTING & GRAPHIC DESIGN • Petr M. Vronský

PUBLISHERS • Masaryk University, Žerotínovo nám. 9, 60177 Brno,
IČO 00216224 & Viella editrice, via delle Alpi 32, I – 00198 Roma

EDITORIAL OFFICE • Seminář dějin umění, Filozofická fakulta
Masarykovy Univerzity, Arna Nováka 1, 60200 Brno

PUBLISHED • 1st edition, 2018

ISBN 978-88-3313-090-3

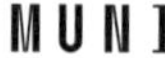

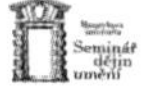

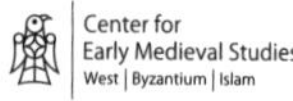

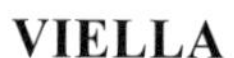

CONTENTS

INTRODUCTION

ANDRÉ · GRABAR PLOTINUS · AND THE · POTENCY · OF LATE · ANTIQUE IMAGES

ADRIEN PALLADINO

Few are probably the scholars of medieval, Byzantine, and Late Antique art history who have never encountered the name of André Grabar (1896–1990) /ILL. 1/.[1] Born in Kiev,

1 For a biographical sketch, see Ivan FOLETTI, "André/Andrej Nikolajevič Grabar", in *Personenlexikon zur Christlichen Archäologie. Forscher und Persönlichkeiten vom 16. bis zum 21. Jahrhundert*, Stefan HEID, Martin DENNERT eds, Regensburg 2012, vol. 1, pp. 601–602. See also Maria Giovanna MUZJ, *Visione e presenza: iconografia e teofania nel pensiero di André Grabar*, Milan 1995 – I refer to the French transl., *eadem*, *Un maître pour l'art chrétien: André Grabar. Iconographie et théophanie*, transl. Charles-André BERNARD, Paris 2005; *Drevnerusskoe iskusstvo. Vizantija i Drevnjaja Rus›. K 100-letiju Andreja Nikolaeviča Grabara (1896–1990)* [Old Russian art. Byzantium and Kievan Rus'. For the 100th-birthday of Andrej Nikolajevič Grabar], Engelina S. SMIRNOVA ed., Saint Petersburg 1999, sp. pp. 9–108; Linda M. ROUILLARD, "Grabar, André (July 26, 1896, Kiev – October 5, 1990, Paris), Archaeologist and Art Historian of Classical Antiquity, Byzantium, and the Middle Ages", in *Handbook of Medieval Studies. Terms, Methods, Trends*, Albrecht CLASSEN ed., Berlin/New York 2010, vol. III, pp. 2320–2323; Marta SERRANO COLL, "André Grabar (1896–1990). The Novel Conception of Iconography", in *Rewriting the Middle Ages in the Twentieth Century*, vol. III: *Political Theory and Practice*, Julia PAVÓN BENITO ed., Turnhout 2015, pp. 197–221.

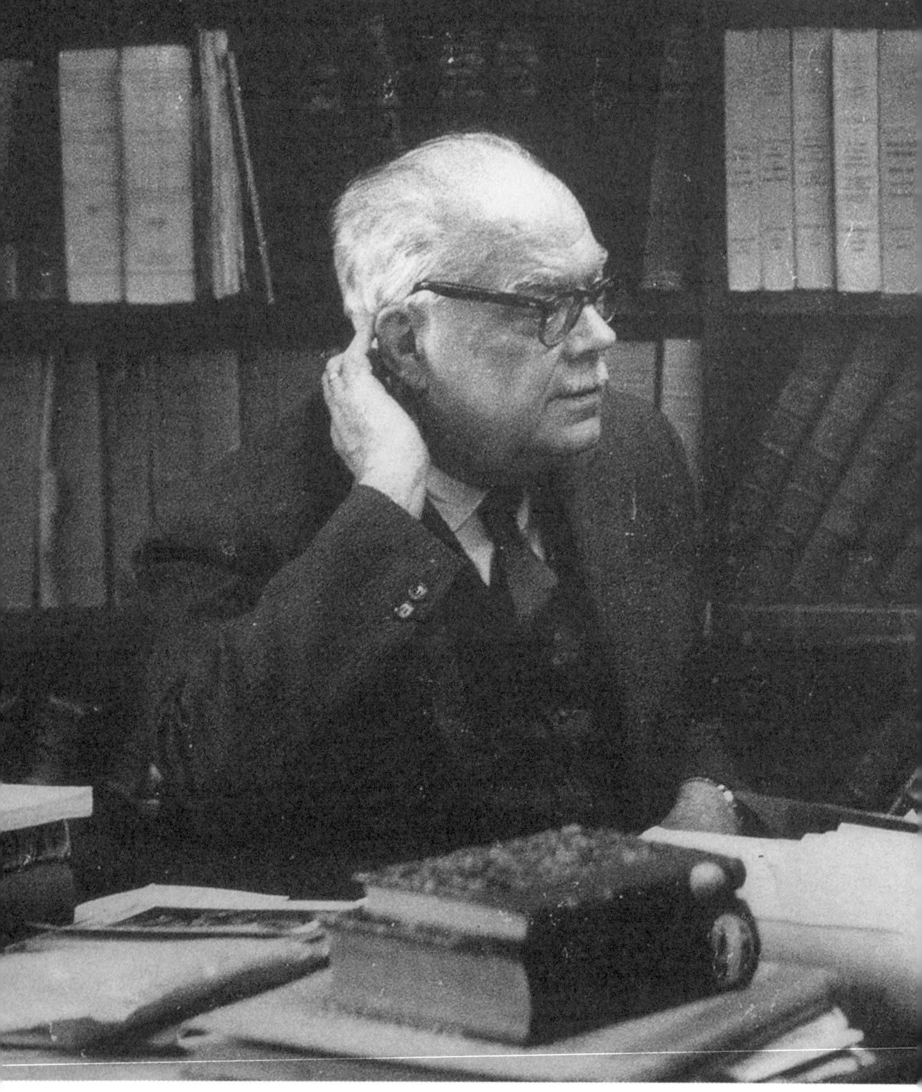

ILL. 1

André Grabar at the Collège de France

in the words of Gilbert Dagron (1932–2015), "[...] the city where Russian Christianity modelled itself on Byzantium and extended Byzantine tradition until us", the origins of Grabar seem to have instinctively led him to study artistic and religious phenomena related to images within the "Byzantine" sphere /ILL. 2/.[2] It is also what his solid Russian formation in Saint Petersburg amongst the first masters of the discipline of Byzantine art history, Nikodim Pavlovič Kondakov (1844–1925) and the latter's students Dimitri Vlas'evič Ajnalov (1862–1939) and Jakov Ivanovič Smirnov (1869–1918) would suggest.[3] However, the political and historical events following the Revolution in 1917 and an exceptional life-course also contributed to make André Grabar a figure deeply embedded between Orient and Occident, and among Byzantinists "[...] without any doubt the one who paid the most attention to the arts of the Latin West".[4] A look at his bibliography confirms this statement: with a preference for "Eastern" or "Byzantine" topics, Grabar nonetheless touched upon an impressive variety of aspects and covered a vast area of geographical territories searching

2 Gilbert DAGRON, "Préface: André Grabar (1896–1990)", in André GRABAR, *Les origines de l'esthétique médiévale*, Paris 1992, pp. 5–10, sp. 5. See also Gilbert DAGRON, "André Grabar et les images", *Comptes rendus des séances de l'Académie des Inscriptions et Belles-Lettres*, CXLIX/3 (2005), pp. 1125–1128; Henry MAGUIRE, "André Grabar. 1896–1990", *Dumbarton Oaks Papers*, XLV (1991), pp. XII–XV.

3 On Kondakov, see Ivan FOLETTI, *Da Bisanzio alla Santa Russia. Nikodim Kondakov (1844–1925) e la nascita della storia dell'arte in Russia*, Rome 2011, pp. 85–172. I refer to the English transl., *idem*, *From Byzantium to Holy Russia. Nikodim Kondakov (1844–1925) and the Invention of the Icon*, transl. Sarah MELKER, Rome 2017; on Ajnalov, Ludmila G. KRUSHKOVA, "Dmitrij Vlas'evič Ajnalov", in *Personenlexikon* (n. 1), vol. 1, pp. 53–54; on Smirnov, *eadem*, "Jakov Ivanovič Smirnov", in *Personenlexikon* (n. 1), vol. 2, pp. 1172–1173.

4 Yves CHRISTE, "André Grabar et l'Occident", *Comptes rendus des séances* (n. 2), pp. 1117–1123, sp. p 1117.

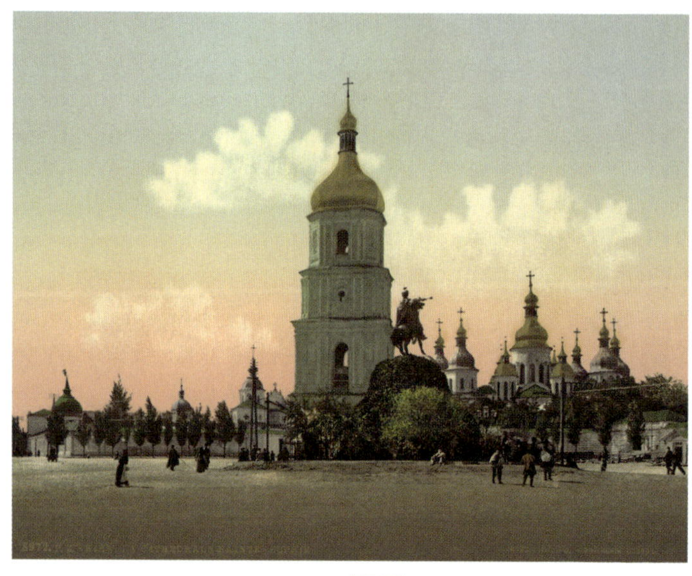

ILL. 2
St Sophia cathedral in Kiev, postcard, c. 1890–1900

for the traces of artistic phenomena of Late Antique and medieval culture.[5]

His attempts at understanding and bridging East and West are not so surprising when one considers that the second part his intellectual formation, from 1922 onwards, was the life of a Russian émigré in France, a path enriched notably by a constant exchange with some of the most eminent French Byzantinists of the time. On the one hand Paul Perdrizet (1870–1938) /ILL. 3/ first at Strasbourg, on the other hand Charles Diehl (1859–1944) and Gabriel Millet

5 Bibliography in Muzj, *Un maître* (n. 1), pp. 253–266.

(1867–1953) in Paris /ILL. 4/.[6] To some extent, despite the hardships of emigrating from Russia to Bulgaria and subsequently to France, Grabar must have felt at home in this new social and intellectual environment. Perdrizet, Diehl or Millet were, just as the Russian teachers of Grabar, part of the first international network of Byzantinists which was discussing questions related to the emergence of Byzantine art, specifically trying to understand the "oriental" or "occidental" part within this genesis.[7] Grabar had, in fact, experienced the best of the two worlds just before they would be separated by revolutions and war.

In the frame of this introduction, I would like to acquaint the reader with one of André Grabar's essential essays, entitled *Plotin et les origines de l'esthétique médiévale*, here translated to English /ILL. 5/.[8] This article was influential in the field

6 On Perdrizet, see Charles PICARD, "Éloge funèbre de M. Paul Perdrizet, membre de l'Académie", *Comptes rendus des séances de l'Académie des Inscriptions et Belles-Lettres*, LXXXII/3 (1938), pp. 270–280; on Millet, see Jean-Michel SPIESER, Judith SORIA, "Millet, Gabriel", in *Dictionnaire critique des historiens de l'art actifs en France de la Révolution à la Première Guerre mondiale*, Philippe SÉNÉCHAL, Claire BARBILLON eds, 2015 [online].

7 On the development and progressive independence of the field of "Byzantine" art history from Christian archaeology at the turn of the century, the bibliography is vast, and no exhaustive monograph exists to this day. See for example *Présence de Byzance*, Jean-Michel SPIESER ed., Gollion 2007; on the *Orient oder Rom?* question at the turn of the century, I indicate only Carola JÄGGI, "Die Frage nach dem Ursprung der christlichen Kunst: Die 'Orient oder Rom' – Debatte im frühen 20. Jahrhundert", in *Giuseppe Wilpert archeologo Cristiano*, Atti del convegno, (Roma, 16–19 maggio 2007), Stefan HEID ed., Rome 2009; *Orient oder Rom? Prehistory, History and Reception of a Historiographical Myth (1880–1930)*, Ivan FOLETTI, Francesco LOVINO eds, Rome 2018 [in press].

8 Originally printed in *Cahiers Archéologiques*, I (1945), pp. 15–34. Reprinted in André GRABAR, *L'art de la fin de l'Antiquité et du Moyen Âge*, 3 vols, Paris 1968, vol. 1, pp. 15–29; *idem*, *Les origines de l'esthétique médiévale*, Paris 1992, pp. 29–57. This

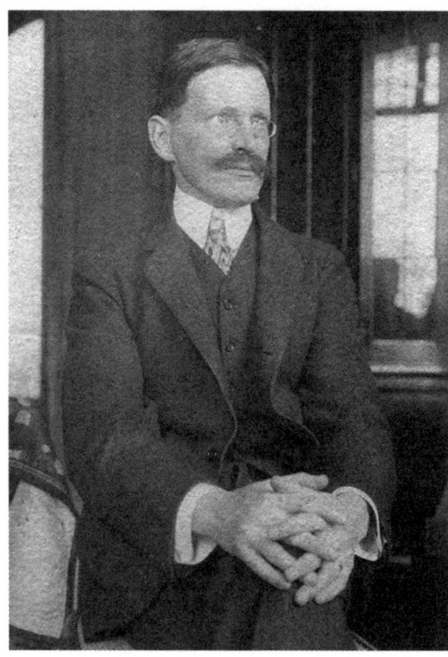

ILL. 3
Paul Perdrizet, 1908

ILL. 4
Gabriel Millet, conference at the Sorbonne

of Late Antique and Byzantine art history not only because of its content, but is also crucial when related to a historiographical framing. In order to present the essay and the figure of Grabar, I would like to follow four leading threads. I will first expound the subject of the text, its reception, its main critiques, and its position in the context of the opus of Grabar. A second moment will be dedicated to the notion of "perspective", pervasive in this essay, which will be contextualised within the rediscovery of the artistic manifestations of

edition, with a foreword by Gilbert Dagron and two other texts on representations of the intelligible in the Byzantine world, also exists in Italian: *Le origini dell'estetica medievale,* transl. Maria Grazia BALZARINI, Milan 2001; and Spanish: *Los orígenes de la estética medieval,* transl. María CONDOR, Madrid 2007.

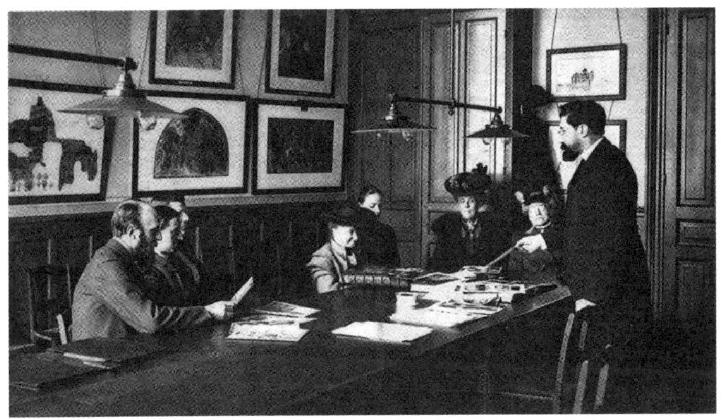

Byzantium. The notion will be related to the Russian context, and more broadly to the "invention" of the Russian icon as both traditional and avant-garde artform at the beginning of the twentieth century. The essay will also be briefly set in the context of the birth of the *Cahiers Archéologiques*, founded at the end of the Second World War as a new platform for art historical exchange. Lastly, I will try to highlight the legacies of the approach taken by Grabar in the essay and relate them to current research focuses of the field of art history, before asking a final question: why translate, and is it still relevant for the twenty-first century observer to view and re-examine Late Antique and medieval art with André Grabar's eyes?

AN "ICONIC" ARTICLE

As the title of the article *Plotinus and the Origins of Medieval Aesthetics* clearly announces, Grabar positioned himself within a specific branch of philosophy: aesthetics. The

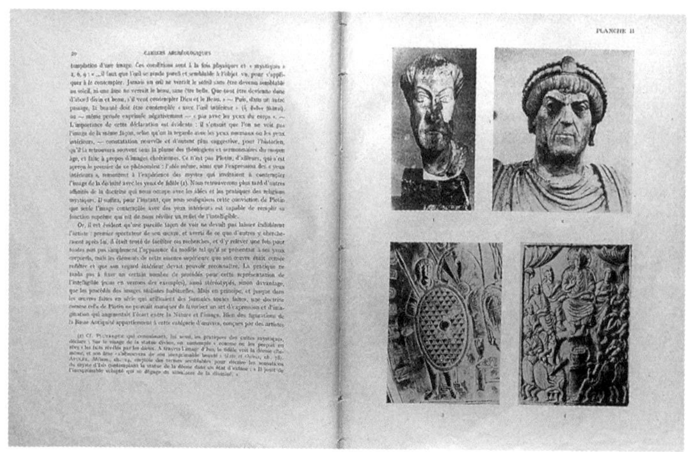

ILL. 5
Page and plate from "Plotin et les origines de l'esthétique médiévale", *Cahiers Archéologiques*, I (1945)

scholar was then forty-nine years old, already a confirmed scholar of the field of Byzantine art history, and one year from his nomination at the Chair of Early Christian and Byzantine Archaeology at the *Collège de France*. In the essay, he chose a very broad subject, the origins of medieval "aesthetics", framing it within a clearly defined body of text, the *Enneads*. The latter were written by Porphyry of Tyre (234–305) in the second half of the third century in order to preserve the thoughts of his master, Neoplatonist philosopher Plotinus (ca 204/205–270). The philosophical thought of Plotinus and Neoplatonic ideas more generally were, since long before the article and until now, applied to and reflected upon in a variety of studies dealing in general with the perception of art or with the representation of the intelligible in particular. The usual breadth of the writings of Plotinus on art, especially his doctrines on the rejection of materiality and the intelligible contemplation of things are, as a matter of fact, used in many different fields, ranging from ancient philosophy to contemporary art theory. As such, the *Enneads* appeared to some scholars as an optimal "blank page" on which ideas – or ideologies – could be laid, according to contexts, epochs, and fields.[9] It is thus no surprise that the theory developed by the Late Antique philosopher has been extensively used in order to explain philosophical, cultural, visual, religious, or aesthetic traits related in particular to early Christianity and to the "Byzantine sphere".[10] Framed specifically in art historical research, the *Enneads* thematise one of the field's transversal questions: the dichotomy between mimesis and reality. According to Plotinus, visual arts do not (or should not) barely imitate visible objects produced by nature but are rather inspired

9 For example, the collective volume *Neoplatonism and Western Aesthetics*, Aphrodite ALEXANDRAKIS, Nicholas H. MOUTAFAKIS eds, Albany, NY 2002; Thomas LEINKAUF, "Überlegungen zum Status des Bildes und der Kunst bei Plotin", in *Zur Erscheinung kommen. Bildlichkeit als theoretischer Prozess*, Anne EUSTERSCHULTE, Wiebke-Marie STOCK eds, Hamburg 2016, pp. 23–36; for the use of Plotinus in the frame of Christian Late Antiquity, see Stéphane BIGHAM, "L'incontro di nuove visioni: la fede Cristiana e Plotino", in *Genealogia dell'immagine Cristiana. Studi sul cristianesimo antico e le sue raffigurazioni*, Daniele GUASTINI ed., Florence/Lucca 2014, pp. 108–121; Pietro DEL SOLDÀ, "Il tramonto di mimesis per Plotino e i primi cristiani", *ibidem*, pp. 122–133; see also Ewgenij V. BARABANOW, "Ästhetik des Frühchristentums", *Theologische Quartalschrift*, CLVI (1976), pp. 259–276; in general on the notion of Early Christian Aesthetics and Plotinus, see Paul Corby FINNEY, "Aesthetics", in *The Eerdmans Encyclopedia of Early Christian Art and Archaeology*, 3 vols, *idem* ed., Grand Rapids 2017, vol. 1, pp. 16–17.

10 For example, *Byzantine Perspectives on Neoplatonism*, Sergei MARIEV ed., Boston/Berlin 2017.

more directly – and thus more perfectly – by intelligible models. Within the possible uses of the textual material inherited from Plotinus, it is specifically this notion related to the representation of the intelligible, the ineffable contact with the Νοῦς (Intelligence or Spirit), that André Grabar was reflecting upon when he published his paper in 1945.[11]

Grabar was indeed looking in Plotinus for a guide. A guide on how to look at Late Antique art, and especially this intelligible aspect, the intellectual as opposed to the sensible vision. In this process, Grabar uses the philosopher to claim that Late Antique and subsequently medieval imagery were much more straightforward in the relationship they established with the beholder. He argues, in fact, that they did not presuppose the addition of successive knowledge but should instead be aiming at direct and total knowledge. This fact is interesting, Grabar goes on, since it could provide us with information on the way images had to be developed by the artists. In order to give access to direct knowledge, they had to invent and settle strict and artificial conventions, which would allow the definition of the sacred by means of the visual arts, in such a way as to give access to the intelligible vision. Before everything else, the article of Grabar therefore speaks about the invention of figurative languages capable to achieve this intention.

It goes without saying that these languages, since they most of the time deliberately refuse to imitate material reality, are also going against the canons established from the

11 On the composite background of the text but the unique tonality binding together the *Enneads*, see Pierre Hadot, *Plotin ou la simplicité du regard*, Paris 1997, sp. pp. 13–22.

sixteenth and throughout the nineteenth century by the incipient field of art history.[12] Considering art as a means of access and not as an end for creating illusion, Grabar asks the reader of the essay to take the philosophical frame composed by Plotinus as an invitation to look differently, or rather – in Plotinian terms – to look "beyond the appearances" of Late Antique art. Approaching artworks in the "[...] philosophical and religious value he [Plotinus] attributes to vision" permits to Grabar to understand not only the shift of aesthetics occurring during Late Antiquity within another paradigm than that of stylistic decadence, but also a shift in the very function of images. To the illusion of presence proposed by classical art, images conceived according to "Plotinian" principles should reproduce essential notions of the intelligible, thus conveying the perception of real presence. This further allowed Grabar to place the focus of his essay not only on the creation of artworks, but also to open to the questions of representation and perception.[13] After this general introduction on the fundamental traits of Plotinian philosophy related to contemplation, Grabar recognises and formulates six principles following Plotinian ideas which should allow,

12 Since Giorgio Vasari (1511–1574), but as an early example, consider the aesthetic criteria of viewing ancient art promoted by Johann Joachim Winckelmann (1717–1768) in the second half of the eighteenth century, see Édouard POMMIER, *Winckelmann, inventeur de l'histoire de l'art*, Paris 2003. For a more general overview of the history of the discipline, see Udo KULTERMANN, *Geschichte der Kunstgeschichte. Der Weg einer Wissenschaft*, 2nd rev. ed., Munich 1996.

13 All crucial questions, for which one can still consult the studies of Ernst H. GOMBRICH, *Art and Illusion: A Study in the Psychology of Pictorial Representation*, New York 1960; on the topic and the term of "representation", so often summoned in art history, see also the important article of Carlo GINZBURG, "Représentation: le mot, l'idée, la chose", *Annales. Économies, Sociétés, Civilisations*, (1991), pp. 1219–1234.

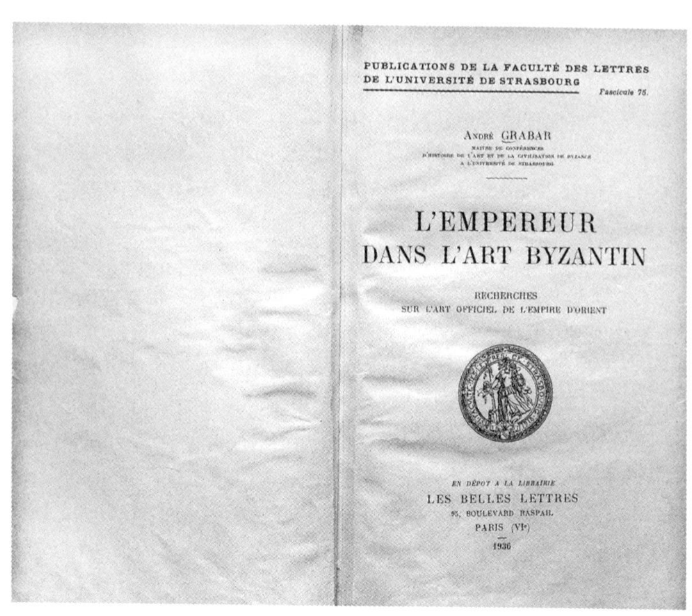

PUBLICATIONS DE LA FACULTÉ DES LETTRES
DE L'UNIVERSITÉ DE STRASBOURG

Fascicule 75.

ANDRÉ GRABAR
MAITRE DE CONFÉRENCES
D'HISTOIRE DE L'ART ET DE LA CIVILISATION DE BYZANCE
A L'UNIVERSITÉ DE STRASBOURG

L'EMPEREUR
DANS L'ART BYZANTIN

RECHERCHES
SUR L'ART OFFICIEL DE L'EMPIRE D'ORIENT

EN DÉPOT A LA LIBRAIRIE
LES BELLES LETTRES
95, BOULEVARD RASPAIL
PARIS (VIe)
1936

ILL. 6
Frontpage of *L'empereur dans l'art byzantin*, Paris 1936

by artistic means, the contemplation of the intelligible. Those principles are the use of the single plane, careful depiction of details, the use of "reverse" and "radiant" perspective, the detachment of characters and objects from the ground plane, their enveloping in light or halos of light, and, lastly, the acute geometrization of nature and figures. Grabar then recognised these principles in a wide variety of artworks, in a large chronological and geographical range, from the second to the ninth century and from the caravan-city of Palmyra to the

Roman church of Santa Maria Maggiore, without forgetting an inevitable detour through Constantinople.

This very broad range in temporality and choice of monuments, linked with the quantity of possible interpretations of Plotinian philosophical thought applied to images, has led to some of the main critiques formulated against Grabar's undertaking. For example, Daniele Guastini wrote, probably to some extent rightly, that Grabar considered only one step of the development of Christian artistic forms, that is the moment related to the earliest forms of "Byzantine art". Guastini then argued that, being Russian, Grabar could consider this "Byzantine" phase as the only true form of Christian art but was however not looking at the earlier phases of its manifestation, the one which was created in continuity with classical Roman tradition:

> Here lies – if we can express it this way – Grabar's mistake: to have believed that the Christian eye was, in fact, the Neoplatonic eye and that everything stemming from Christianity which was not belonging to this culture was a step on the way of decadence of ancient art. In this way, but at another level, he reintroduced the classicist idea of decline.[14]

In another line, one of the main critiques of Grabar's essay was formulated in 1951 by Panayotis A. Michelis in an article on the aesthetics of Byzantine art. According to

14 Daniele GUASTINI, "Aux origines de l'art paléochrétien", *Images Re-vues*, VII (2009), [online]; Guastini also came back to the question of the representation of the invisible in *idem*, "Voir l'invisible. Le problème de l'*eikon* de la philosophie grecque à la théologie chrétienne", *Images Re-vues,* VIII (2011), [online].

Michelis, Grabar had turned Plotinus' "[...] metaphysics into physics" and ascribed him "[...] intentions and suggestions on technique, of which he himself must have been utterly unaware".[15] Grabar however clearly underlined in the article that: "It goes without saying that the ideas of Plotinus exerted absolutely *no influence* on the activity of the artists of his time and of the following epoch." Further, when the essay on Plotinus was reprinted in a collection of his articles published in 1968, it was inserted in a section titled "Doctrine and Ideas", where Grabar clarified once again that the philosopher is but "[...] a particularly discerning witness and *not the actual inspirer* of medieval art".[16] As framed by Grabar, Plotinus has thus to be understood not strictly as a theoretician of medieval aesthetics, but rather as a guide who can help not only to understand the genesis of Christian art but also the various shifts in aesthetics between the classical Antique and the Early Christian world. But not all of the art of this period, since, as Guastini remarks, Grabar in some sense excluded for example the art of the catacombs or of the sarcophagi created in continuity with the Roman world. Rather, he looked especially towards the potency of certain kinds of images and their ability to ease or achieve a presentification of the intelligible.

---

15 Panayotis A. Michelis, "Neo-Platonic Philosophy and Byzantine Art", *The Journal of Aesthetics and Art Criticism*, xi/1 (1952), pp. 21–45, sp. p. 36; Muzj, *Un maître* (n. 1), p. 176.

16 Grabar, *L'art de la fin de l'Antiquité* (n. 8), vol. 1, pp. 5–111, sp. p. 5. The 1968 miscellany, containing ninety articles printed between 1917 and 1966, is particularly interesting in that it contains several of Grabar's texts translated into French which had previously been only available in Russian.

The other point on which Grabar was contested is related to a question he expanded upon on different occasions, and which lies also at the core of the article here translated: the question of the power and frontality of images. Grabar had already widely discussed his opinions on the origins and specific potential of frontal images in the publication which first brought him renown, *L'empereur dans l'art byzantin* (1936) /ILL. 6/.[17] In this book, he stated a filiation, or at least an impact, of Late Antique imperial representations and Early Christian art of the Constantinian and later eras. The thesis was most notably rebutted by Thomas F. Mathews in *The Clash of Gods* (1993).[18] Mathews notably stressed the fact that Grabar was born in Russia in 1896 under the reign of the last Tsar Nicholas II (r. 1896–1917), to a father who was senator and as such an official of the imperial regime. More specifically because of the already-mentioned monograph on imperial art, which was followed by the chairing of a 1950-Symposium at the Dumbarton Oaks Centre in Washington entitled "The Emperor and the Palace", Mathews suggested that Grabar and other scholars who had witnessed the downfall of imperial dynasties, could have nourished what he called a "[...] nostalgia for lost empire".[19] Having emigrated, Mathews argued, Grabar could only entertain this feeling, which would have naturally led him to express theories about this continuity and preponderance of imperial art within the new Christian frame. These pages of Mathews

17 André GRABAR, *L'empereur dans l'art byzantin. Recherches sur l'art officiel de l'Empire d'Orient*, Paris 1936.

18 Thomas F. MATHEWS, *The Clash of Gods. A Reinterpretation of Early Christian Art*, Princeton, NJ 1993, pp. 16–22; 2nd rev. ed. Princeton, NJ 1999.

19 *Ibidem*, p. 19. See also MUZJ, *Un maître* (n. 1), pp. 178–191.

stirred controversy and provoked many discussions, some of them particularly lively.[20] Mathews' assumption indeed seems too univocal, as no trait of Grabar's work point towards this form of imperial nostalgia. More interestingly for the argument developed here, it has to be noted that Grabar arrived at questions relative to the representations of images conveying power not exclusively through the lens of imperial iconography. As in the article here translated, he also did so through questions pertaining to the representation of the true reality as expressed in Neoplatonic thought, but also through the study of spaces and images accompanying the cult of martyrs especially in his other great two-volume study *Martyrium* (1946) /ILL. 7/.[21] The latter and the article on Plotinus were conceived and written during the war and are indeed closely related, as Grabar himself stated.[22] They are especially tied together on the important question of the "face-to-face" encounter with the image and the divinity itself, whose roots, Grabar argues, are to be found in the mystery religions of "Eastern" divinities like Isis-Osiris,

20 Mathews' reception has been discussed in a preface to the Italian translation, see Eugenio Russo, "Per leggere 'The Clash of Gods. A Reinterpretation of Early Christian Art' di Thomas F. Mathews", in *Scontro di Dei. Una reinterpretazione dell'arte paleocristiana*, transl. Alessandro Dell'Aira, Eugenio Russo, Milan 2005, pp. IX–L; see also Anne-Orange Poilpré, "Bilan d'une décennie de réactions à l'ouvrage de Thomas F. Mathews, *Clash of Gods*, Princeton, 1993", *Antiquité tardive*, XIII (2005), pp. 377–385.

21 André Grabar, *Martyrium. Recherches sur le culte des reliques et l'art chrétien antique*, 2 vols, Paris 1946. Grabar came back to this study, reacting to the remarks of several Anglo-Saxon authors in *idem*, "Martyrium ou 'vingt ans après'", *Cahiers archéologiques*, XVIII (1968), pp. 239–244. On the relationships between the text on Plotinus and *Martyrium*, see also Muzj, *Un maître* (n. 1), pp. 125–129.

22 Already in the text about Plotinus; Grabar, *Martyrium* (n. 21), II, pp. 192–193, n. 4; *idem*, *L'art de la fin de l'Antiquité* (n. 8), vol. 1, p. 5.

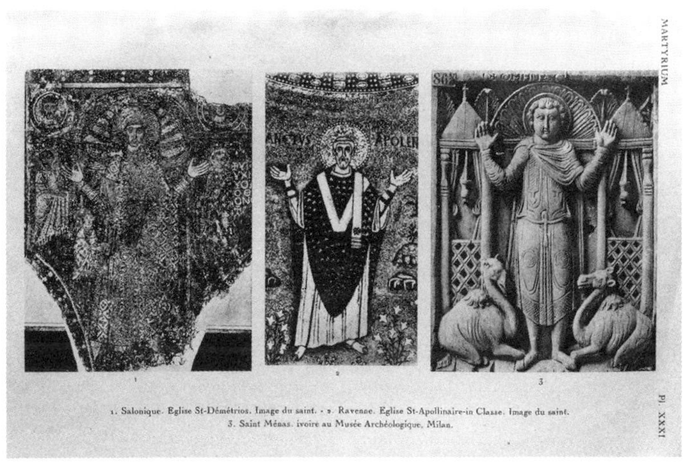

ILL. 7
Plate XXXI from *Martyrium. Recherches sur le culte des reliques et l'art chrétien antique*, Paris 1946

Attis, or Mithras.[23] This is where we come across a search for the origins of the tradition of Christian cult image, which, according to Grabar was first taken from religious manifestations peculiar to the Levant, Egypt, or Syria, within what he calls "the half-Greek, half-local art practised there". In any case, the goal (and power) of such images lies in the immediate contemplation of the divinity through the vision of images and on the central notion of the use of the "eyes of the mind". We come back to this question later, but it is clear that the chain of thought started by Grabar with the

23 These questions can be found, further developed, in GRABAR, *Martyrium* (n. 21), II, pp. 133ff and some years later by Ulrich RAPP, *Das Mysterienbild*, Münsterschwarzach 1952.

study of these topics is closely related to what has been called the "power", "performance", or "agency" of images.[24] The study of these phenomena related to images would result for Grabar in researches on the possible negation of this power, a notion which he studied in particular by focusing on a key-moment of struggle with images: the Byzantine iconoclasm /ILL. 8/.[25]

It is therefore within this fundamental frame of understanding the presence of power or divinity through images that the three main books of Grabar on the representations of the emperors, the martyrs, and on Iconoclasm have to be inscribed.[26] The brief text on Plotinus appears as a very coherent way to access the dense and permanently stimulating corpus on images developed by Grabar over the years. A brief outline of his research focuses also shows that Mathews was mistaken to reduce its frame only to the imperial aspects of

24 David FREEDBERG, *The Power of Images. Studies in the History and Theory of Response*, Chicago 1991. Freedberg's position proposed an interpretative key based on psychology and ethnology, in which the "oriental icon" is presented as the exact type of "non-artistic" image. About this, see also the remarks of Michele BACCI, "Vieux clichés et nouveaux mythes: Constantinople, les icônes et la Méditerranée", *Perspective*, II (2012) [online]; on agency, the seminal work is Alfred GELL, *Art and Agency: An Anthropological Theory*, Oxford 1998; see Matthew RAMPLEY, "Art History and Cultural Difference: Alfred Gell's Anthropology of Arts", *Art History*, XXVIII/4 (2005), pp. 524–551; Caroline VAN ECK, *Art, Agency and Living Presence: From the Animated Image to the Excessive Object*, Berlin 2015.

25 André GRABAR, *L'iconoclasme byzantin. Dossier archéologique*, Paris 1957; 2nd revised and augmented edition, Paris 1984.

26 These three topics also touch upon the crucial question of material incarnation as the crucial notion related to the creation of images in Christianity, an element paradoxically going against the supposed aversion for the visible of the first Christians, see for example Georges DIDI-HUBERMAN, *L'image ouverte. Motifs de l'incarnation dans les arts visuels*, Paris 2007, sp. pp. 98ff.

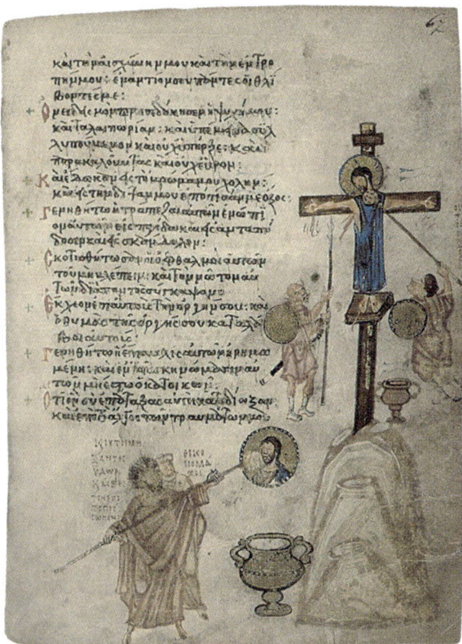

ILL. 8
Iconoclasts, from the Chludov Psalter, ca 850–875, fol. 67r, Constantinople / Moscow, State Historical Museum, MS D. 129

Late Antique art. Even a re-reading of *L'empereur dans l'art byzantin*, with all the flaws that time has dredged up, does not appear to be the ideologically-biased book of a Russian émigré nostalgic for a lost empire.[27] I would even add that if there really is something "Russian" within André Grabar's work, it is surely elsewhere, perhaps in this attention for presence through and of cult images, that one should look for it.

27 A conception which is perpetuated, for example, by DEL SOLDÀ, "Il tramonto" (n. 9), pp. 128–133; on Grabar and Russian art, another topic than the one addressed here, see for example Engelina S. SMIRNOVA, "Andrej Nikolaevič Grabar i voprosy russkoj kul'tury v ego naučnom nasledii", [Andrej Grabar and Problems of Russian Culture in his Scholarly Heritage], in *Drevnerusskoe iskusstvo* (n. 1), pp. 76–82; Olga MEDVEDKOVA, "André Grabar et la filiation entre l'art antique, l'art byzantin et russe ancien dans l'historiographie russe", *Revue des études slaves*, LXXXVII/1 (2016) [online].

In his art historical formulation of the principles recognised in Plotinus, Grabar is part of a discourse initiated at the beginning of the twentieth century by theoreticians of art history, which was still looking to establish itself as an objective science. Grabar indeed brings back a lot of Plotinus' philosophical questions specifically for the use of perspective and its different modalities. Particularly in the above-mentioned principles recognised in Plotinus, Grabar identifies two types of construction of space: "radiant" and "reverse" perspective. The latter especially has a long conceptual history which was certainly not unfamiliar to the scholar which had been formed in Saint Petersburg.[28] In reading this essay, this term deserves to be contextualised in a more closely historiographical perspective, since it lies at the intersection between scientific discourse and philosophical-theological implications on how to look at images. This point is relevant to the historiography of art history in general and Byzantine art specifically, while also being linked with questions related to the rediscovery of the

28 The notion has notably been studied by Rudolf ARNHEIM, "Inverted Perspective in Art: Display and Expression", *Leonardo*, V/2 (1972), pp. 125–135; Clemena ANTONOVA, "On the Problem of 'Reverse Perspective': Definitions East and West", *Leonardo*, XLIII/5 (2010), pp. 464–469; *eadem*, *Space, Time, and Presence in the Icon: Seeing the World with the Eyes of God*, Ashgate 2009; Clemena ANTONOVA, Martin KEMP, "'Reverse Perspective': Historical Fallacies and Alternative View", in *The Visual Mind II*, Michelle EMMER ed., Cambridge, Mass. 2005, pp. 399–431; see also Christopher R. LAKEY, "Review of: Clemena Antonova, *Space, Time* (n. 28) and *Visualizing Medieval Performance: Perspectives, Histories, Contexts*, Elina GERTSMAN ed., Aldershot 2008", *Oxford Art Journal*, XXXIV/2 (2011), pp. 287–309.

Russian icon in the first two decades of twentieth century, a phenomenon most indebted to Nikodim P. Kondakov.[29] I do not wish to enter too deeply into a topic which has been extensively researched, but I would like to try highlighting some elements and explain how Grabar maybe indirectly suggests a link between Late Antique art and the contemplation of icons.[30]

To start, it is interesting to note that one of Grabar's "Western" teachers, Gabriel Millet, as early as 1899, in his study on the twelfth-century mosaic decoration of the Daphni monastery in central Greece, analysed the different types of perspectives

---

29 See notably Nikodim P. KONDAKOV, "O naučnyx zadačax istorii drevne--russkogo iskusstva" [On the scientific objectives of the history of ancient Russian art], in *Pamjatniki drevnej pismennosti i iskusstva* [Monuments of ancient writing and art], Saint Petersburg 1899, pp. 1–47; Pavel MURATOV, "Russkaja živopis' do serediny XVII veka'" [Russian painting up to the mid seventeenth century], in *Istoria russkogo iskusstva* [History of Russian Art], Igor E. GRABAR ed., Moscow 1914, vol. IV, pp. 5–406; Also after his exile, see the important work on the Icon, first published in abridged English edition, Nikodim P. KONDAKOV, *The Russian Icon*, Oxford 1927; *idem*, *Russkaja Ikona* [The Russian Icon], 4 vols, Prague 1928–1933; On the context, see FOLETTI, *From Byzantium* (n. 3); see also Wendy SALMOND, "Ellis H. Minns and Nikodim Kondakov's *The Russian Icon* (1927)", in *Modernism and the Spiritual in Russian Art. New Perspectives*, Louise HARDIMAN, Nicola KOZICHAROW eds, Cambridge 2017, pp. 165–194.

30 Xénia MURATOVA, "La riscoperta delle icone russe e il 'revival' bizantino", in *Arti e storia del Medioevo*, vol. IV: *Il Medioevo al passato e al presente*, Enrico CASTELNUOVO, Giuseppe SERGI eds, Turin 2004, pp. 589–606; Xénia MURATOVA, "Per la storia dell'arte medievale in Russia. Gli inizi: collezionisti, amatori, scrittori, eruditi, editori, primi storici d'arte", in *Medioevo: arte e storia*, (Atti del convegno internazionale di studi, Parma, 18–22 settembre 2007), Arturo C. QUINTAVALLE, Parma 2008, pp. 120–130; *eadem*, "Pavel Muratov historien d'art en Occident", in *La Russie et l'Occident. Relations intellectuelles et artistiques au temps des révolutions russes*, Ivan FOLETTI ed., Rome 2010, pp. 65–95; Ivan FOLETTI, "L'exposition des icônes de 1913 à Saint-Pétersbourg: la découverte des origines chrétiennes russes", in *Re-thinking, Re-making, Re-living Christian Origins*, Ivan FOLETTI [*et al.*] eds, Rome 2018, pp. 323–330.

adopted by "Byzantine" artists.[31] Combining these types, increasing height and receding lines, Millet argues that probably, "[...] the mosaicist of Daphni had some notions of linear perspective [...]; in fact he places the skyline very high or employs two perspectives: the view of Jerusalem seems to be taken in bird's-eye-view."[32] Further, we understand that this use of perspective is negatively connotated for Millet, as it reveals that the Byzantine artist was no longer able to understand the Antique way of using perspective: "The Byzantines, having returned to the first tradition, inherited the methods of Pompeii, without attaching any price to it, without understanding their meaning. They used them with a lordly clumsiness [*une maladresse de grands seigneurs*]."[33] It is the same "depreciative" use of "reverse" perspective as that in Dimitri V. Ajnalov's dissertation "Ellinističeskie osnovy vizantiiskogo iskusstva" [The Hellenistic Origins of Byzantine Art] (1900).[34] In this text the Russian scholar, pupil of Kondakov and teacher of Grabar, wanted to prove that the classical tradition was transmitted to posterity and thus preserved by Byzantine art. However, taking note of a problematic use of perspective in the compositions illuminated in the tenth-century Ečmiadzin Gospels, Ajnalov

31 Gabriel MILLET, *Le monastère de Daphni. Histoire, architecture, mosaïques,* (Monuments de l'art byzantin, 1), Paris 1899.

32 *Ibidem*, p. 99.

33 *Ibidem*, p. 103.

34 Dimitri V. AJNALOV, "Ellinističeskie osnovy vizantiiskogo iskusstva. Issledovanija v oblasti rannevizantiiskogo iskusstva", *Zapiski Imperatorskogo Russkogo Arkheologičeskogo obščestva*, n. s. XII, 3–4 (1900–1901). Widely made available, with a preface by Cyril Mango, more images and extended by marginal notes of Ajnalov himself only in 1961 as *idem*, *The Hellenistic Origins of Byzantine Art*, Cyril MANGO ed., transl. Elizabeth SOBOLEVITCH, Serge SOBOLEVITCH, New Brunswick 1961.

argued that "[...] in this particular case one might be inclined to ascribe this to incompetent draughtsmanship or to the use of reverse perspective",[35] before trying to understand the possible architectural origins of the illuminations. When applied to Late Antique or Byzantine art at the turn of the century, the question of reverse perspective is associated to a lack, or rather to a loss, of skill of the artists: they are deemed unable to make correct foreshortenings while following the Hellenistic models.

However, a change to this notion seems to arrive in the same years. The first to coin the term of "reverse perspective" was the Byzantinist Oskar Wulff (1864–1946).[36] In an essay titled "Die umgekehrte Perspektive und die Niedersicht" [The inverted perspective and the low eye level perspective] (1907) /ILL. 9/, he used the term to characterise different types of perspectives used sometimes concurrently by ancient art: bird's-eye-view, frontal view, and, interestingly, "inner contemplation" (*innere Anschauung*). The latter is actually the same as what Grabar describes as "radiant".[37] Wulff goes on to argue that these types of perspectives dominated a whole millennium of Byzantine artistic tradition. The most important

35 AJNALOV, *The Hellenistic Origins* (n. 34), pp. 100–104.

36 Martin DENNERT, "Oskar Constantin Wulff", in *Personenlexikon* (n. 1), vol. 2, pp. 1332–1333. Wulff was also an important protagonist in the *Orient oder Rom* debate, and a friend of Josef Strzygowski, see Barbara SCHELLEWALD, "Der Blick auf den Osten – eine Kunstgeschichte à part. Oskar Wulff und Adolph Goldschmidt an der Friederich-Wilhelms-Universitat und die Folgen nach 1945", in *In der Mitte Berlins: 200 Jahre Kunstgeschichte an der Humboldt-Universität*, Horst BREDEKAMP, Adam S. LABUDA eds, Berlin 2010, pp. 207–228.

37 Oskar WULFF, "Die umgekehrte Perspektive und die Niedersicht. Eine Raumanschauungsform der altbyzantinischen Kunst und ihre Fortbildung in der Renaissance", in *Kunstwissenschaftliche Beiträge August Schmarsow gewidmet*, Heinrich WEIZSÄCKER [*et al.*] eds, Leipzig 1907, pp. 1–40.

general conclusion we can draw considering the modalities of representation, Wulff says, is that "[...] the real signification of a form of representation can only be deciphered through psychological analysis".[38] His examination of the continuity and discontinuity of "reverse perspective" further confirmed for the scholar on the one hand that the "*Völkerpsychologie*" could be used as a methodological tool in art history – going against the idea of a purely individual artistic creation –, on the other confirms the "[...] law of continuity of all development of art".[39] Uniting a psychological approach and positivist art history, Wulff in this sense demonstrates that he was truly a man of the beginning of the nineteenth century. As pointed out by Clemena Antonova and Charles Lock,[40] Wulff's essay was never well received in Germany, probably because of its dismissal in the famous essay "Die Perspektive als 'symbolische Form'" [Perspective as Symbolic Form], published in German in 1927 by Erwin Panofsky (1892–1968) and based on a rebuttal of Wulff's theses formulated by mathematician Karl Doehlemann (1864–1926) in 1910.[41] Doehlemann argued that art ignorant of the idea of linear perspective (as

---

38 WULFF, "Die umgekehrte Perspektive" (n. 37), p. 33.

39 *Ibidem*. For some notions on *Völkerpsychologie*, see Wan-Chi WONG, "Retracing the footsteps of Wilhelm Wundt: explorations in the disciplinary frontiers of psychology and in Völkerpsychologie", *History of Psychology*, XII/4 (2009), pp. 229–265.

40 ANTONOVA, "On the problem" (n. 28); Charles LOCK, "What is Reverse Perspective and who was Oskar Wulff? Essay-review of: Antonova, *Space, Time* (n. 28) and Avril PYMAN, *Pavel Florensky: A Quiet Genius. The Tragic and Extraordinary Life of Russia's Unknown da Vinci*, London/New York 2010", *Sobornost. Eastern Christian Review*, XXXIII/1 (2011), pp. 60–89.

41 Erwin PANOFSKY, "Die Perspektive als 'symbolische Form'", in *Vorträge der Bibliothek Warburg. Vorträge 1924–1925*, Fritz SAXL ed., Leipzig/Berlin 1927, pp. 258–330; Karl DOEHLEMANN, "Zur Frage der sogenannten 'umgekehrten Perspektive'", *Repertorium für Kunstwissenschaft*, XXXIII (1910), pp. 85–87.

developed in the early modern period most notably by Leon Battista Alberti) cannot, a fortiori, act within an intellectual frame of "reversing" this perspective.

Instead it was shown that "reverse perspective" was popularised by the writings of Pavel Florensky (1882–1937) /ILL. 10/, the "Russian Da Vinci", who wrote specifically about the viewing of Russian icons.[42] His text, "Obratnaja perspektiva" [Reverse Perspective], has a long history. It stems from a lecture given in 1920 in Moscow, but was only published in 1967, three decades after the death of its author in the prison camp of Solovki.[43] Florensky's text deals with important questions developed on many levels during those years in Russian intellectual circles. Art historical theoretical discourse was in opposition to the idea of time and space, and perspective was therefore a question at the heart of the conceptualisation of images and much discussed.[44] Some Russian theoreticians, such as Vladimir Favorsky (1886–1964), relying on the use of reverse perspective, defined the "Byzantine" plane as the only one on which time could be configured by simultaneously making visible the past and present, lateral and distant aspects of objects – thus linking theological and pictorial aspects of icon paintings.[45] Florensky, in his essay,

42 On Florensky, see PYMAN, *Pavel Florensky* (n. 40).

43 Pavel FLORENSKY, "Obratnaja perspektiva", *Trudy po znakovim sistemam*, III (1967), pp. 381–416. English translation as "Reverse perspective (1920)", in Pavel FLORENSKY, *Beyond visions. Essays on the Perception of Art*, Nicoletta MISLER ed., transl. Wendy SALMOND, London 2002, pp. 197–272. On this history of the text, *ibidem*, pp. 199–200; ANTONOVA, *Space, Time* (n. 28), *passim*; Nadia PODZEMSKAIA, "'La vision est aussi un art': le débat sur l'espace dans la Russie soviétique du début des années 1920 et l'enseignement aux Vhutemas", *Ligeia*, LXXIII–LXXVI (2007), pp. 132–149, sp. pp. 145ff.

44 *Ibidem*.

45 *Ibidem*, p. 149.

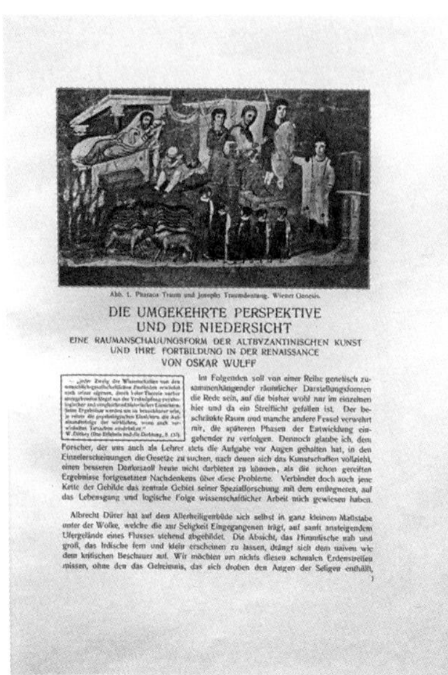

Abb. 1. Pharaos Traum und Josephs Traumdeutung. Wiener Genesis.

DIE UMGEKEHRTE PERSPEKTIVE
UND DIE NIEDERSICHT
EINE RAUMANSCHAUUNGSFORM DER ALTBYZANTINISCHEN KUNST
UND IHRE FORTBILDUNG IN DER RENAISSANCE
VON OSKAR WULFF

Im Folgenden soll von einer Reihe genetisch zusammenhängender räumlicher Darstellungsformen die Rede sein, auf die bisher wohl nur im einzelnen hier und da ein Streiflicht gefallen ist. Der beschränkte Raum und manche andere Fessel verwehrt mir, die späteren Phasen der Entwicklung eingehender zu verfolgen. Dennoch glaube ich, dem Forscher, der uns auch als Lehrer stets die Aufgabe vor Augen gehalten hat, in den Einzelerscheinungen die Gesetze zu suchen, nach denen sich das Kunstschaffen vollzieht, einen besseren Dankeszoll heute nicht darbieten zu können, als die schon gereiften Ergebnisse fortgesetzten Nachdenkens über diese Probleme. Verbindet doch auch jene Kette der Gebilde das zentrale Gebiet seiner Spezialforschung mit dem entlegeneren, auf das Lebensgang und logische Folge wissenschaftlicher Arbeit mich gewiesen haben.

Albrecht Dürer hat auf dem Allerheiligenbilde sich selbst in ganz kleinem Maßstabe unter der Wolke, welche die zur Seligkeit Eingegangenen trägt, auf sanft ansteigendem Ufergelände eines Flusses stehend abgebildet. Die Absicht, das Himmlische nah und groß, das Irdische fern und klein erscheinen zu lassen, drängt sich dem naiven wie dem kritischen Beschauer auf. Wir möchten um nichts diesen schmalen Erdenstreifen missen, ohne den das Geheimnis, das sich droben den Augen der Seligen enthüllt,

ILL. 9
Page from Oskar Wulff, "Die umgekehrte Perspektive und die Niedersicht", 1907

therefore considered perspective as a fundamental question not only of artistic theory, but also of the understanding of the world in general. His central question of geometry and perspective is how to represent intelligible *reality*. The artist, he argues, "[...] depicts not an object, but the life of the object, according to the impression he receives of it."[46] Thus he does not passively reproduce what he is looking at, but a synthesis of his impressions, emotions, memories, ideas. This most perfect form of artistic creation becomes apparent, Florensky considers, in "[...] icons that transgress the laws of perspective".[47] In this sense, reverse perspective is not the

46 Florensky, "Reverse perspective" (n. 43), p. 269.

47 *Ibidem*, p. 202.

mistake of naïve artists who forgot naturalistic tradition but becomes "an organic and dynamic counter conception to linear perspective".[48]

Without delving too deeply into Florensky's text, it is difficult not to make a more or less direct association with the ideas that we can find developed by Grabar and the anti-mimetic vision he recognises in Plotinus. And indeed, it is not only in this Russian intellectual context that Grabar was educated, but the writings of Florensky and others had awakened the more general interest of scholars, avant-garde painters, and amateurs to what was, in those years, being rediscovered as the Russian image *par excellence* – the icon.[49] This rediscovery of the "primitives" was accompanied, as several scholars have already demonstrated, in the years following the turn of the twentieth century, by a more general deconstruction of perspective "[...] by Cézanne, Picasso, Braque and not less important ideological deconstruction with the introduction of new terms".[50] We also know the crucial role that the art historian Nikodim P. Kondakov /ILL. 11/,

48 Fabian HEFFERMEHL, "Wi-Fi in Plato's Cave: The Digital Icon and the Phenomenology of Surveillance", in *Digital Orthodoxy in the Post-Soviet World. The Russian Orthodox Church and Web 2.0*, Mikhail SUSLOV ed., Stuttgart 2015, pp. 83–110, sp. p. 96.

49 On these questions, see FOLETTI, "L'exposition" (n. 30); *idem, From Byzantium* (n. 3), pp. 85–169. The title of the English edition highlights this notion of "Invention of the Icon" which is one of the epicentres of Kondakov's heritage; see also Geraldine LEARDI, "'Tout est dans la mesure': Matisse davanti alle icone russe nel 1911", in *La Russie et l'Occident* (n. 30), pp. 11–30; Rémi LABRUSSE, "Byzance et l'art moderne. La référence byzantine dans les cercles artistiques d'avant-garde au début du XXe siècle", in *Présence de Byzance* (n. 7), pp. 55–89.

50 HEFFERMEHL, "Wi-Fi" (n. 48), p. 96; François-René MARTIN, "Le moine-peintre et le primitif. L'invention des 'Primitifs' russes dans une perspective internationale", *Cahiers du monde russe*, LIII/2–3 = *L'invention de la Sainte Russie: l'idée, les mots et les images* (2012), pp. 1–11; FOLETTI, "L'exposition" (n. 30).

Grabar's professor, played in this rediscovery of medieval Russian art and specifically the "traditional" form of the icon.[51] It is further interesting to note that in the years 1915 to 1922, when the third volume of Kondakov's *Ikonografija Bogomateri* [Iconography of the Mother of God] was being completed, Grabar was in Sofia with Kondakov. In this volume, dedicated to the iconography of the *Theotokos* in Italy from the twelfth to the sixteenth century, Kondakov wrote much that was in harmony with the judgments and theories of Florensky, especially on the role of Giotto in the loss of the canons established by the Second Nicaean council (787) and the progressive integration of the *perspectiva artificalis* in "Western" art.[52] Giotto is indeed often credited by the earliest historiographers such as Cennino Cennini, Lorenzo Ghiberti, or Giorgio Vasari, with the surpassing of the old *maniera Graeca* and the opening to a "modern" way of painting. On the contrary, Kondakov's judgment defended a strongly orthodox point of view.[53] In the book, he characterised Giotto as being "unable" to paint true devotional image, icons. This is in particular true for figures, but more so in the figuration of spaces, which he describes prior to Florensky, but in very similar terms, as a "theatrical mise-en-scène" good for dec-

51 Foletti, *From Byzantium* (n. 3), pp. 85–169.

52 On the theology of image, see Christoph von Schönborn, *L'icône du Christ. Fondements théologiques élaborés entre le Ier et le IIe Concile de Nicée (325–787)*, Fribourg 1976; for a historiographical perspective on Nicaea II and icons, see Gilbert Dagron, *Décrire et peindre. Essai sur le portrait iconique*, Paris 2007, pp. 65–82; more closely relating to perspective, I would also like to point out to the rich pages of Jean Clair, *Méduse. Contribution à une anthropologie des arts visuels*, Paris 1989, pp. 89–104.

53 Ivan Foletti, "Nikodim Pavlovitch Kondakov, *Iconographie de la mère de Dieu*: le manuscrit retrouvé", in Nikodim Kondakov, *Iconographie de la mère de Dieu*, Roma 2011, pp. XXXIX–XLVI.

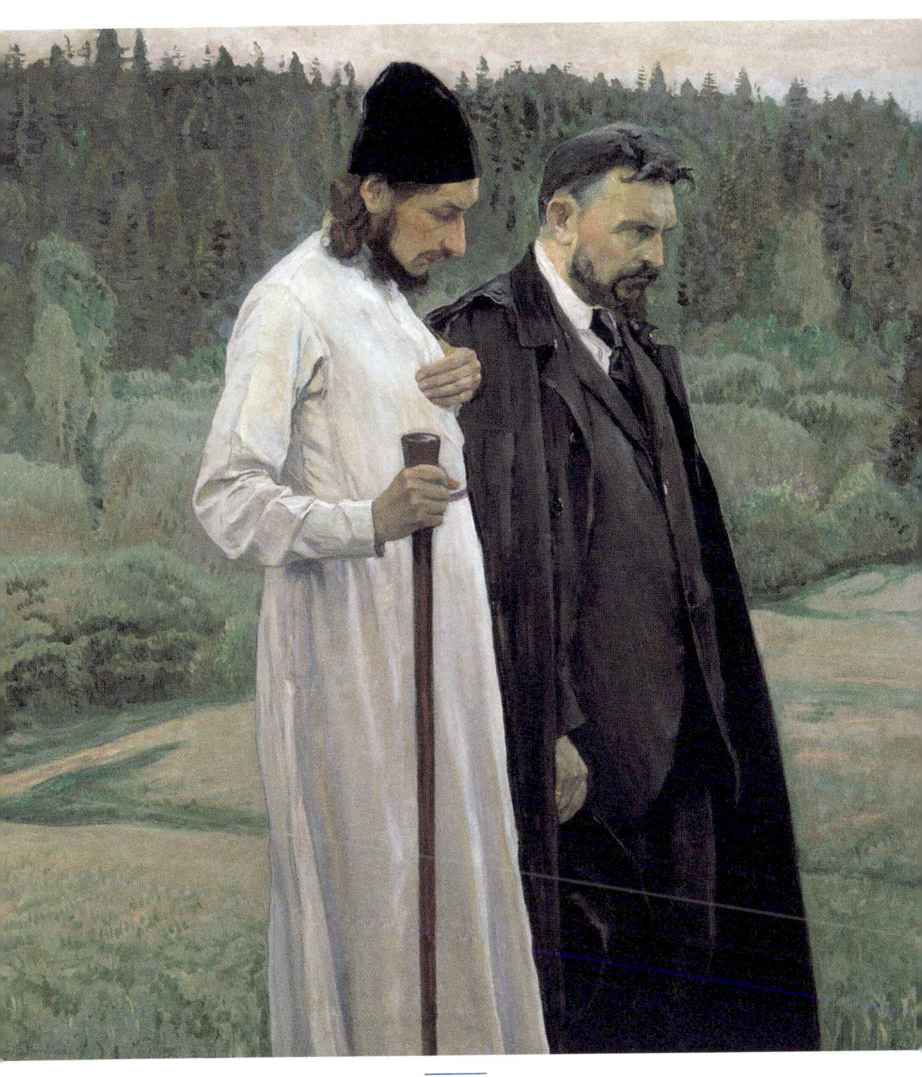

ILL. 10

Mikhail Nesterov, Portrait of Pavel Florensky and Sergei Bulgakov, oil on canvas, 1917 / Moscow, Tretyakov Gallery

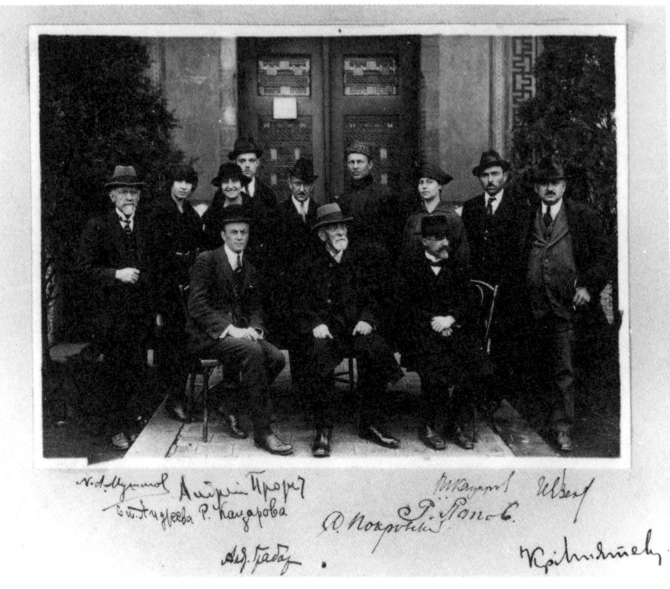

ILL. 11
Nikodim P. Kondakov surrounded by friends and students, on the back, fourth from the left André Grabar, 1921

orative works but not the pious contemplation of images.[54] According to Kondakov, the Italian Renaissance had certainly brought good painters, but also an apparent decadence of "true" and "efficient" religious artforms and cultic images.[55] It is thus clear that it were not only ideas and a general "aesthetic" rediscovery which emigrated to the West with scholars

54 Foletti, "Nikodim Pavlovitch Kondakov" (n. 53), p. xliii.

55 On anti-Renaissance orthodox sentiment, see Vittorio Strada, "Icona e anti-icona. Armonia e caos nella spiritualità russa", in *Il mondo e il sovra-mondo dell'icona*, Sante Graciotti ed., Florence 1998, pp. 71–81.

and avant-garde painters, but also, with figures quickly bridging the two worlds like André Grabar, a profound historical knowledge and perception of cultic images.[56] This knowledge was, furthermore, indissociably linked with religious contexts and practices surrounding them.

I would like to mention one last uncanny link between Plotinus' thought and the Russian icon. When Grabar writes that this "[...] more abstract language of art had to bend to defined conventions" in order to deliver its direct efficacity, he speaks about the fixation of iconographic traits and visual elements in a very similar way envisaged by the Greek and Russian orthodox iconographic traditions. These strict, dogmatic elements, which seem so diametrically opposed to the notion of individual inspiration of the artist that was promoted since the early modern period, had already struck Adolphe-Napoléon Didron (1806–1867) when he discovered the icon ateliers at Mount Athos in 1839.[57] The shaping of the languages "spoken" by cult images, especially in the earliest phases of their development, were of deep interest to André Grabar, who made it his life's work to understand

56 Ivan Foletti, "Nikodim Pavlovitch Kondakov et Prague: comment l'émigration change l'histoire (de l'art)", *Opuscula historiae artium*, LXIII (2014), pp. 2–10.

57 *Manuel d'iconographie chrétienne grecque et latine*, intr. and notes by Adolphe-Napoléon Didron, transl. Paul Durand, Paris 1845, pp. XII–XVII. See Hans Belting, *Bild und Kult. Eine Geschichte des Bildes vor dem Zeitalter der Kunst*, Munich 1990, pp. 28–30; see also Catherine Brisac, Jean-Michel Leniaud, "Adolphe-Napoléon Didron ou les média au service de l'art chrétien", *Revue de l'art*, LXXVII (1987), pp. 33–42; Ivan Foletti, "Tra classicismi e avanguardie. La ricezione dell'estetica bizantina in Francia e in Russia a cavallo tra Otto e Novecento", in *Phantazontes: visioni dell'arte bizantina*, Valentina Cantone, Silvia Pedone eds, Padua 2013, pp. 175–255.

these languages.[58] Again, in Plotinus (but these are ideas already present in Plato and Plutarch), he found a perfect description of what images should aim for:

> It is what the Egyptians had understood, writing not with letters forming sounds and sentences, but with signs *of which each is a science*, a wisdom, a real thing *grasped at once*, and not a reasoning or deliberation. [p. x, v, 8, 5]

The very idea of the use of Egyptian scripture resonates with the thinking of another important protagonist of the debates around the rediscovery the Russian icon, the theologian and philosopher Sergej Nikolaevič Bulgakov (1871–1944) /ILL. 10/.[59] The latter, some years after Florensky, in a text from 1930 on the veneration of the icon, wrote:

> Things without prototype are blind (naturalism). And prototypes without things are empty or abstract (schematism). The creative act of art, making an icon of something, consists first of all in perceiving its prototype through it, and then imprinting it through its own means. *Icons are a hieroglyph of the ideal prototype*, not a repetition or a copy [...], but rather the imprint of the authentic, first image

58 This interest of the scholar in the shaping of iconographic languages and their use by artists between Late Antiquity and the Middle Ages is also the subject of his monograph: André GRABAR, *Les voies de la création en iconograhie chrétienne. Antiquité et Moyen Âge*, Paris 1979. The first part of this book, on Late Antiquity, was already known to English readers prior to the publication of this French edition since it came directly from the Andrew W. Mellon Lectures in the Fine Arts given by Grabar in 1961 in the United States and published as *idem*, *Christian iconography: a study of its origins*, Princeton 1968.

59 FOLETTI, *From Byzantium* (n. 3), pp. 142–144, 224–226.

which, through the representation of it, has a real prototype in the world.[60]

Very significantly, we can see how Bulgakov's statement enters in resonance with the philosophical thought of Plotinus. Bulgakov himself had written on the Greek philosopher on some occasions, but it is here specifically the link with the question of the Incarnation, once again the real presence as opposed to the illusion, that must be emphasised and reframed in Grabar's thought.[61]

As representations of a true reality, icons – just as the first Christian art for Grabar – called on the one hand for a detachment from the materiality, on the other attached the presence of the sacred to this very materiality. In his studies on the notions of the power, presence or agency of Late Antique and medieval images, Grabar – whilst being very broad in his approach – remained focused on the veneration of images such as icons, making theophany and hierophany possible, and on the understanding of the religious phenomena linked with images, throughout his life. Grabar, as a painter himself, may have been even more sensitive to the question of how to achieve a certain vision by using material tools – and not only in cult-images. It is perhaps in this fascination for the potency of the image, its possibility to materialise a true

60 Sergei BULGAKOV, *Ikona i Ikonopočitanie. Dogmatičeskij očerk* [The icon and its veneration. A dogmatic overview], Paris 1931; French ed.: *L'icône et sa vénération. Aperçu dogmatique*, trans. by Constantin E. ANDRONIKOF, Lausanne 1996; transl. here to English by Sarah MELKER from FOLETTI, *From Byzantium* (n. 3), p. 143, my emphasis.

61 Bulgakov writes on the Plotinian conception of the vision of matter in his *Svet nevechernij* [Unfading Light] 1917, pp. 245–247. Transl. in Sergei BULGAKOV, *Towards a Russian Political Theology*, Rowan WILLIAMS ed., pp. 113–162, sp. p. 128.

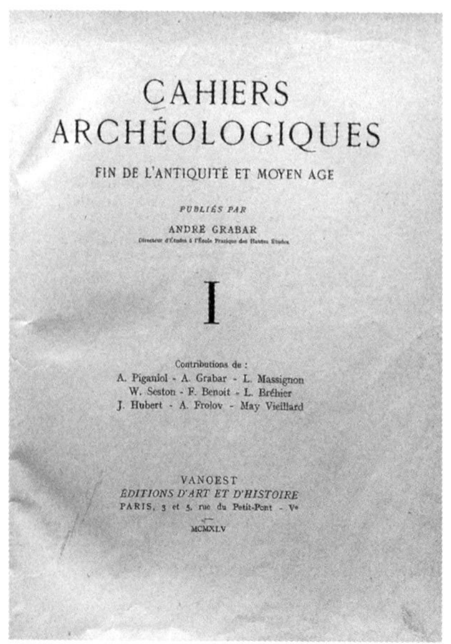
CAHIERS
ARCHÉOLOGIQUES

FIN DE L'ANTIQUITÉ ET MOYEN AGE

PUBLIÉS PAR

ANDRÉ GRABAR

I

Contributions de :
A. Piganiol - A. Grabar - L. Massignon
W. Seston - F. Benoit - L. Bréhier
J. Hubert - A. Frolov - May Vieillard

VANOEST
ÉDITIONS D'ART ET D'HISTOIRE
PARIS, 3 et 5, rue du Petit-Pont - V^e

MCMXLV

ILL. 12
Frontpage of the first issue of the *Cahiers Archéologiques*, 1945

vision, inserted within this briefly sketched intellectual frame, that the Russian origins and formation years of Grabar could shed some light on his understanding of ancient religious art.

A MANIFESTO FOR THE *CAHIERS ARCHÉOLOGIQUES*

The article translated here must also be considered in the context of its publication. As the first article written by André Grabar in the first issue of the *Cahiers Archéologiques* he had founded in 1945, the text has programmatic value /ILL. 12/. The text is one of Grabar's three first published articles in the very first issue of the *Cahiers Archéologiques* and is accompanied by two other essays – one on Syrian liturgy, the other on Visigothic frescoes – testifying to an underlying wish of "uniting" the Eastern and Western medieval world.[62] Furthermore, the article on Plotinus not only speaks about the images' capacity to offer a passage from the sensible to the intelligible, but also suggests a way of looking at images, maybe, if I may suggest, as a way to reopen the "inner eyes" to beauty after the times of the war.

Despite the fact that French Byzantinists, as Grabar himself noted, were far from idle during the Occupation and the War, the founding of a periodical in 1945 strikes as a significant gesture.[63] The article on Plotinian vision must then also be read as an open invitation to discover and rediscover topics and images that would be presented throughout the pages of the periodical. Further, as noted in a review of the first issue by Pierre Courcelle, the new journal, with its eloquent subtitle *Fin de l'Antiquité et Moyen Âge* [End of Antiquity and the Middle Ages] arrived just on point to fill a gap, since it also allowed a focus on this "long-neglected" moment of transition between Antiquity and the Middle Ages.[64] But it did so as well because at the very heart of the enterprise lay what we would now call a deeply interdisciplinary approach. The *Cahiers Archéologiques* proposed to give a large place to "[...] archaeological investigations which

62 André GRABAR, "Une fresque visigothique et l'iconographie du silence", *Cahiers Archéologiques*, I (1945), pp. 124–128; *idem*, "Les ambons Syriens et la fonction liturgique de la nef dans les églises antiques", *ibidem*, pp. 129–133.

63 On French Byzantine studies during the war, see André GRABAR, "La byzantinologie française pendant la guerre: 1940–1945", *Byzantion*, XVII (1944–1945), pp. 431–438.

64 Pierre COURCELLE, "Review of: *Cahiers archéologiques, fin de l'Antiquité et Moyen-Âge*, t. 1; publiés par A. Grabar, 1945", *Revue des Études Anciennes*, XLVIII/3–4 (1946), pp. 298–300.

will consider artistic documents as testimonies on the history of ideas and religious beliefs".[65] In this, once again, we can recognise André Grabar's characteristic methodology, and his deep interest for the religious factor behind monuments: artworks without a function were only of marginal interest within this approach.

The *Cahiers Archéologiques* became, in a short period of time, one of the leading publications in the field of medieval art history and are still published today. In 1952, Grabar had integrated Jean Hubert (1902–1994) to the *Cahiers*, who was not at all a Byzantinist, further opening the journal to works on the "Western" world.[66] In this sense, the role of the journal was not unlike the one which was held by another periodical, founded during the Interwar period by other students of Kondakov, also émigrés, in Prague: *Seminarium Kondakovianum*, bearing the same name as the institute in Prague, and published for the first time in 1927 /ILL. 13/.[67] It is

65 COURCELLE, "Review of: *Cahiers archéologiques*" (n. 64), p. 298.

66 On Hubert, see Alain ERLANDE-BRANDENBURG, "Jean Hubert (1902–1994)", *Bibliothèque de l'école des chartes*, CLIII/2 (1995), pp. 583–588.

67 See Zuzana SKÁLOVÁ, "Das Prager Seminarium Kondakovianum, später das Archäologische Kondakov-Institut und sein Archiv (1925–1952), *Slavica Gandensia*, XVIII (1991), pp. 21–43; Jiří ROHÁČEK, "The Archive of the Institute of N. P. Kondakov", *Convivium*, I/1 (2014), pp. 219–221; Francesco LOVINO, "Leafing through Seminarium Kondakovianum, I. Studies on Byzantine Illumination", *Convivium*, III/1 (2016), pp. 206–213; Ivan FOLETTI, "Nikodim Kondakov, Russia and Czechoslovakia. Byzantine Studies, the Link between East and West", in *From Kondakov to Hans Belting Library. Emigration and Byzantium – Bridges between Worlds*, Ivan FOLETTI, Francesco LOVINO, Veronika TVRZNÍKOVÁ eds, Brno 2018, pp. 18–37; esp. Francesco LOVINO, "*Seminarium Kondakovianum, Byzantinoslavica.* A Comparison", *ibidem*, pp. 38–55; See also Marina DMITRIEVA, "Towards a Transnational History of Russian Culture: The N. P. Kondakov Institute in Prague", in *Transcending the Borders of Countries, Languages, and Disciplines in Russian Émigré Culture*, Christoph FLAMM [*et al.*] eds, Cambridge 2018, pp. 173–198.

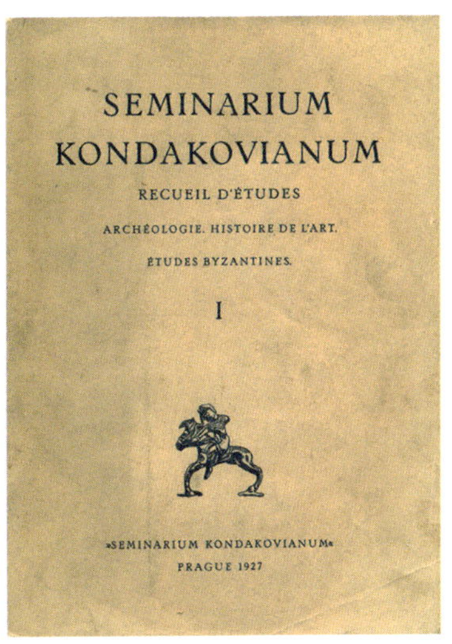

ILL. 13
Frontpage of the first issue of *Seminarium Kondakovianum*, 1927

in this sense no surprise that just five years after the last issue of *Seminarium* in 1940 and after the war, the *Cahiers* took up the flame, proposing a new interdisciplinary journal and platform of discussion between East and West.

WHY TRANSLATE?

Before leaving the reader to the discovery or rediscovery of the text, I would like to underline why seventy-three years after its original publication and twenty-eight years after the passing of its author (1990), this short essay of André Grabar might make sense more than ever.

Firstly, the topics that Grabar touched upon in this article are at the core of art historical research. In a world where digitised images are omnipresent, the deeper understanding of the notion of presence within images – what has been defined for example by Hans Belting as "iconic presence" – seems on the one hand fundamental.[68] On the other hand, the corpus of Grabar opens to questions that have become integral to studies on the potentialities of images within a more and more anthropological approach: notions such as the representation of the intelligible, spiritual seeing, eyes of the mind, theophanic visions and their expectations in Late Antiquity but also a questioning of the ontological status of images, emphasised by Grabar through the lens of Plotinus, have become topical issues of Late Antique and medieval art history.[69] Furthermore, Grabar was in general questioning the power of images, in their capacity to act on us, and in us, but also, not only in religious contexts, to become as such

68 BELTING, *Bild und Kult* (n. 57); *idem*, *Bild-Anthropologie. Entwürfe für eine Bildwissenschaft*, Munich 2001; *idem*, "Iconic Presence. Images in Religious Traditions", *Material Religion*, XII/2 (2016), pp. 235–237. See Roland BETANCOURT, "Medieval Art after Duchamp: Hans Belting's *Likeness and Presence* at 25", *Gesta*, LV/1 (2016), pp. 5–17; on presence in representations and artefacts, see also the comprehensive overview in the volume *Presence. The Inherence of the Prototype within Images and Other Objects*, Robert MANIURA, Rupert SHEPHERD eds, Aldershot 2006, esp. the introduction with bibliography, pp. 1–30. The question of Belting's conception of the *Kultbild*, the cult-image, has been widely discussed since the 1990s. See *Intellektualisierung und Mystifizierung mittelalterlicher Kunst. "Kultbild": Revision eines Begriffs*, Martin BÜCHSEL, Rebecca MÜLLER eds, Berlin 2010.

69 Herbert L. KESSLER, *Spiritual Seeing. Picturing God's Invisibility in Medieval Art*, Philadelphia 2000; *Seeing the Invisible in Late Antiquity and the Early Middle Ages*, Giselle DE NIE, Karl F. MORRISON eds, Turnhout 2005; *The Mind's Eye. Art and Theological Argument in the Middle Ages*, Jeffrey F. HAMBURGER, Anne-Marie BOUCHÉ eds, Princeton 2006; *Looking Beyond. Visions, Dreams and Insights in Medieval Art and History*, Colum HOURIHANE ed., Princeton, NJ 2010; Caroline Walker BYNUM, *Christian Materiality; An Essay on Religion in Late Medieval Europe*, New York 2011; Tobias FRESE, *Aktual- und Realpräsenz. Das eucharistische Christusbild von der Spätantike bis ins Mittelalter*, Berlin 2013; Armin F. BERGMEIER, *Visionserwartung. Visualisierung und Präsenzerfahrung des Göttlichen in der Spätantike*, Wiesbaden 2017.

"embodied".[70] Choosing an approach that was not only formalist, Grabar opened the door to a different understanding of what was often considered a failure in rendering illusionism, addressing new questions to the "first" medieval images, specifically to the perception and use of cultic images.[71] Driven by his background and interests, Grabar wrote about how to look at images, paving the way to a new understanding of the gaze. In this sense, he also indirectly pointed to the interaction of the beholder with artworks, to the relationships between images and religious behaviours, the performative aspects of images, and towards the "iconic" and "synaesthetic" turns of the discipline, which demonstrate a gradual emancipation from pure visuality still expressed in Grabar's article.[72]

Finally, in his description of a certain model of "behaviour" towards images, Grabar had a far-reaching eye. It led him to Palmyra, as he described a sculptural relief depicting a group of veiled women. In this rhythmical composition, executed in a peculiar style, he saw an art "[...] which foreshadows, it seems, the characters of Romanesque sculpture". This relief

70 Most famously, FREEDBERG, *The Power* (n. 24); for other approaches, for example Horst BREDEKAMP, *Theorie des Bildakts: Frankfurter Adorno-Vorlesungen 2007*, Berlin 2010.

71 David HORNUFF, *Bildwissenschaft im Widerstreit: Belting, Boehm, Bredekamp, Burda*, Munich 2012.

72 Bissera V. PENTCHEVA, *The Sensual Icon. Space, Ritual, and the Senses in Byzantium*, University Park, pp. 209–210; *eadem*, "Glittering Eyes: Animation in the Byzantine *Eikōn* and the Western *Imago*", *Codex Aquilarensis*, XXXII (2016), pp. 209–236. See also the important studies of Alexej M. LIDOV, *Ierotopia: sozdanie sakral'nyx prostranstv v Vizatnii i Drevnej Rusi = Hierotopy: The Creation of Sacred Spaces in Byzantium and Medieval Russia*, Moscow 2006. For a convenient overview of the question, see *Iconic Turn: Die Neue Macht der Bilder*, Hubert BURDA, Christa MAAR eds, Cologne 2004; Keith MOXEY, "Visual Studies and the Iconic Turn", *Journal of Visual Culture*, VII/2 (2008), pp. 131–146.

was sculpted on the portico surrounding the cella of the temple of Bel in Palmyra and was dynamited by the so-called Islamic State on the 28th of August 2015 /ILL. 14/.[73] In the conclusion of an essay published as an echo to the destructions in Palmyra, the historian Paul Veyne described the sculptures and reminded us that:

> [...] they were much discussed in the times of Malraux and the great archaeologists of the day: of course, we must mention the contemporary boldness of avant-garde painters and the beginnings of abstract art. What is probable, in any case, is that in Palmyra, the sculptor, standing before the many stylisations made possible by Orient and Occident, took the opportunity to entertain himself by inventing a new one.[74]

And indeed, the article of Grabar should, in these years, be reframed in the context of André Malraux and his impact on the French intellectual world.[75] It seems that through the gaze of Plotinus, Grabar was in a sense also looking at a personal "imaginary museum" of images, composed within his own historiographical gaze, his own *Univers des formes* /ILLS. 15–16/ – a link which is of course not only abstract, since Grabar wrote two volumes of the famous collection directed by Malraux, both on Late Antiquity and early Byz-

73 Christiane DELPLACE, "Palmyre", *Perspective. Actualité en histoire de l'art*, 1 (2017), pp. 9–12.

74 Paul VEYNE, *Palmyre. L'irremplaçable trésor*, Paris 2015, p. 141; translated as: *Palmyra. An Irreplaceable Treasure*, transl. Teresa L. FAGAN, Chicago 2017.

75 Walter GRASSKAMP, *André Malraux und das imaginäre Museum. Die Weltkunst im Salon*, Munich 2014.

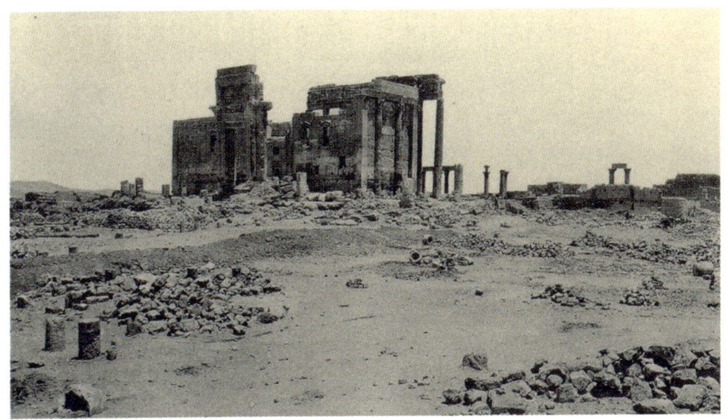

ILL. 14
Temple of Bel, Palmyra, plate from *La Syrie antique et médiévale illustrée*, René Dussaud, Paul Deschamps, Henri Seyrig eds, Paris 1931

antine art.[76] He considered medieval art to be a dialogue, a dialogue with images but also, such as his guide Plotinus, a dialogue with oneself. As an émigré, Grabar did not seem to express much resentment towards exile, nor did he seem to withdraw to an inner retreat, perhaps because he knew so many different cultures of the medieval and Late Antique worlds. Once again in the words of Paul Veyne, "truly, to know and have the wish to know only one culture, one's own, is to condemn oneself to live under a candle snuffer."[77]

76 André GRABAR, *Le premier art Chrétien*, Paris 1966; *idem*, *L'Âge d'or de Justinien. De la mort de Théodose à l'Islam*, Paris 1966.
77 VEYNE, *Palmyre* (n. 74), p. 141; see also Finbarr Barry FLOOD, "Between Cult and Culture: Bamiyan, Islamic Iconoclasm, and the Museum", *The Art Bulletin*, LXXXIV/4 (2002), pp. 641–659.

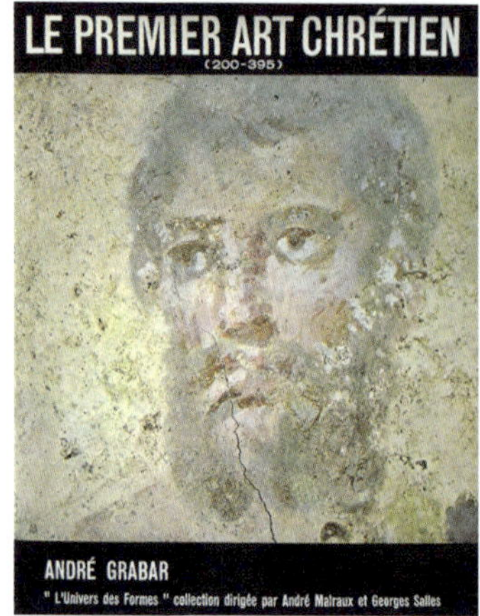

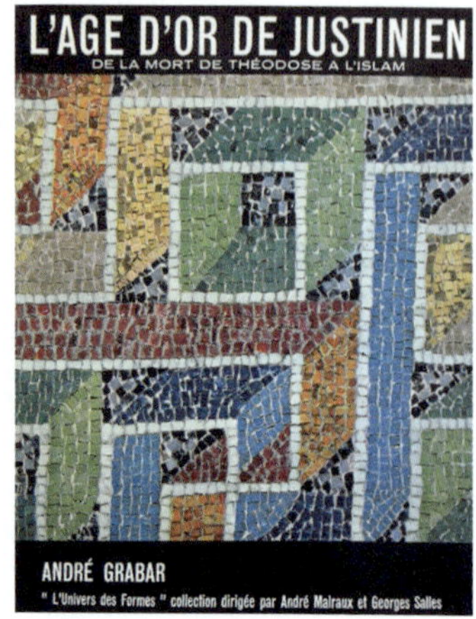

ILLS 15–16
Covers of André Grabar, *Le premier art chrétien*, Paris 1966 and *L'âge d'or de Justinien*, Paris 1966; collection "L'Univers des formes"

To conclude in the same direction, I can only speak of translation (and reproduction) as the means to fight the violence against images and culture. It is with the wish of making a constant dialogue possible and some further steps towards the understanding of the potency and beauty of artistic phenomena of ancient art that the present introduction, translation, and reproduction of this text were conceived. Discovering or rediscovering through the translation this beautiful text of Grabar is a way of giving the possibility to reframe tradition and acknowledge the beauty of images – and not only those of Palmyra, whose now lost patrimony is reproduced here.

ARTICLE OF ANDRÉ GRABAR

PLOTINUS·AND THE·ORIGINS OF·MEDIEVAL AESTHETICS

ANDRÉ GRABAR

This essay does not pretend to be a counterpart to the excellent short book of Pierre-Maxime Schuhl, *Plato and the art of his times*.[1] The author of that publication treats his subject as a historian of philosophy. He writes of an author who, many times over, had to define his attitude towards the art of his time, an attitude that could all the more be defined that it was connected, on the one hand, to the entire philosophical work of Plato, on the other hand, to an art which left behind numerous and well-studied artworks. We know quite precisely the successive steps of the fast and progressive evolution of Athenian art in the times of Plato, and Schuhl was able to show towards which aspects of this art, to which phases of its evolution, the preferences of the philosopher were going,

1 Pierre-Maxime SCHUHL, *Platon et l'art de son temps*, Paris 1933. [*Note of the editor*: regarding the bibliographical apparatus, footnotes have been unified, when necessary extended to the full quote for more precision].

and which art he actually considered when he assigned to it a determined role in his philosophical doctrine.

It is as an art historian, and not as a historian of philosophy, that I will try to examine some of the texts of Plotinus. Despite their extent, the *Enneads* offer only few passages where it is immediately question of contemporary artworks. Anyhow, in many ways, the art of the middle of the third century, like it was practiced in the times of Plotinus (205–270), is not comparable to Athenian art in the times of Plato. In Egypt, where Plotinus spent his youth, as well as in Italy, where he resided afterwards, wherever the philosopher might have observed it, this art was living against the background of traditions and models bequeathed by the prior epoch. Instead of evolving progressively according to a curve defined by new creations, as in the times of Plato, it oscillated between different styles (*manières*), to which the fashion of the day alternatively gave preference, but which all took their starting point in the work of a more ancient school of art, Hellenistic, classical, nay archaic.

These procedures of course did not exclude spontaneous creations, nor more or less original currents, both in the provinces of the Empire and in the capital where the best artists of the times converged. In the field of portraiture notably, which the Romans had been developing for centuries, the personality of the artists and, at least, the taste of the epoch, are sufficiently clear to discern. But even in this domain, and, more so in works of art less closely tied to the direct imitation of Nature, it is – in the third century – the influence of monarchs and their court who had a decisive impact on a significant part of artistic production. The unremitting changes on the throne of the August resulted in no less frequent changes of orientation of art in the capital and in some provincial workshops. In short, rather than following an evolution fed by internal reasons specific to it, the art of the time of Plotinus transformed constantly and, so to speak, in zigzag, but without ever departing from the tradition handed down by the great eras of Greek art.[2]

Therefore, to know which aspect of such hesitant and impersonal art the sympathies and critiques of a writer of this period favoured, it would have been necessary for Plotinus to have specifically named these artworks – but he did not – and the sculptures and paintings about which he was thinking to have been conserved. Yet, the majority of the artistic works of this time have vanished or remain unidentified in the heap of late Roman monuments conserved in collections of the two worlds. On this point as well, consequently, it would not be possible to take up, for Plotinus and the art of his time, an investigation which would be a counterpart to the study of Schuhl. And for that matter, the aesthetic insignificance of most works of art known from the third century does not engage to extensive research in this direction.

In fact, it is not the attitude of Plotinus towards the art he knew that should be considered, but his way of contemplating an artwork, and the philosophical and religious value he attributes to vision. With the opinions he expressed on the appropriate way to study the work of art, to interrogate

2 On the art of the third century, see the excellent summary by Gerhart RODENWALDT, "The Transition to Late-Classical Art. I. From Septimus Severus to Elagabalus", in *The Cambridge Ancient History*, vol. XII, London 1939, chap. XVI, pp. 544–570. For sculpture: Charles PICARD, *La sculpture antique de Phidias à l'ère byzantine*, vol. II, Paris 1926, pp. 453ff.

and to enjoy each vision and in particular the contemplation of an artistic creation, Plotinus foreshadows the medieval beholder. And it is the anticlassical medieval forms which seem to best correspond to this new programme whose characteristics Plotinus was the first to outline. One will not be surprised to see, within art history, this role of precursor attributed to Plotinus, in whom historians of thought and of natural sciences have often seen early signs of the medieval mind.[3] The observations I will make thus square with the way in which, besides, the Plotinian work was situated in relation to the Middle Ages; and if since until now, aside from the many studies on the aesthetics of Plotinus, one has never thought to draw links between his writings and certain facts of art history, it is certainly only due to the lack of curiosity for the artistic creation of the late Roman Empire and to the small number of studies which, until recent times, have been dedicated to the artistic history of this period. Recent works have partly bridged this gap[4] and have brought our attention to the aesthetics of works contemporary to Plotinus, or shortly posterior, which precisely provide points of comparison with the doctrine of the philosopher.

A remarkable passage in the *Fourth Ennead* (IV, 3, 11) will teach us, once and for all, what Plotinus expects of a work of art:

> The wise men of old who wanted to make the Gods present to them by constructing temples and statues seem to

3 Émile BRÉHIER, *La Philosophie de Plotin*, Paris 1928, pp. 145–146.

4 Bibliography in RODENWALDT, "The Transition" (n. 2), pp. 778–779. See also the two albums dedicated to the art of the fourth, fifth, and sixth centuries, by Hayford PEIRCE and Royall TEYLER, under the improper title: *L'Art byzantin*, Paris 1932 and 1934.

> have rightly seen the nature of universe; they understood that it is always easy to *attract the universal soul*, but that it is particularly easy to retain it, by constructing an object disposed to be subjected to its influence and to *receive its participation*. Yet, the figured representation of a thing is always disposed to *endure the influence of its model*, it is like a mirror capable to seize its appearance.[5]

The image is a mirror of the represented thing which, as such, pertains to its model, in virtue of the stoic principal of universal sympathy. This mirror serves not only to reflect the appearance of material things, but also and above all to capture the universal soul, that is the spiritual essence of these things and even divinity. For Plotinus, the superior principle, the Νοῦς (Intelligence or Spirit), achieves the union of all cosmic realities, whereas it is precisely the phenomenon of sympathy uniting the different parts of the visible world that is a weakened image of this perfect union. Each thing is provided with a soul, the entire universe is animated, and this soul, present in each material thing, is none other than the reflection of the Νοῦς – the superior Intelligence. Moreover, this reflection of Νοῦς, this spiritual element, is the *only real thing* that can be found. The rest is pure matter, that is to say, empty non-being.

Animated in this way, the material world is surely justified and valorised: through it, one acquires the knowledge of Intelligence. But, on the other hand, the Intelligence it reflects

5 Original translations from Émile Bréhier, *Ennéades*, 7 vols, Paris 1924–1938. Emphasis by André Grabar. The translations presented here are mine, based on the text of Bréhier.

is the only reality in matter. The work of art will, as a mirror, have to reflect this matter as well. But it will be useful only as instrument of knowing the Νοῦς (an imperfect yet useful instrument): this is the *raison d'être* of a work of art. What it can offer to us, what is appropriate to look for in it, is the reflection – weakened but certain – of the supreme Intelligence, of Intelligence – the sole reality.

It is easy to predict the repercussions that such ideas could have on the practice of figurative arts. They might have brought doubt on the value of representations which had no other mission than to imitate the appearance of things of Nature. In the long run, they were capable of diminishing the sensibility of the artist – and of the beholder – for the characteristics of a compromised material world. In search of the essence of things, both could become accustomed to letting their gaze slide over their appearance, and to note fewer facts worthy of being kept in mind than their predecessors. Their viewing experience risked diminishing, whilst the search for the "true" image, that of the intelligible, inevitably committed them to submit direct vision to a more or less energetic interpretation. To remain intelligible, however, this more abstract language of art had to bend to defined conventions. Plotinus himself had considered this matter.

In fact, if the reason for the existence of a work was as Plotinus wanted it (and not merely the pleasure of the beauty it realises, nor the imitation of appearances of material things, nor the moral or intellectual instruction that its subject can bring), the beholder could not discern the lesson it conveys without special preparation. The viewer had to be informed about the physical nature of vision:

> "Whence does it come from that distant objects seem smaller and smaller and that, at a great distance, appear to be at a not so considerable interval, whilst the neighbouring objects are seen with their *true size* and at their *true* distance? Do objects seem smaller because the light tends to gather toward the eye and adjust to the size of the pupil?
>
> Is it that, the more the matter of the visible object is distant, the more the form arrives to the eye isolated from the matter? [...] Or is there a magnitude which covers the space and that we perceive as it really is at each point where it is? It ought to that *the object itself be near the eye*, in order to be *known in its true size*. [...]
>
> But there is in colours and forms a common character: it is the reduction which, for colours, is erasing, for the size, diminution; and size diminishes in proportion of the erasing of colour. It is what becomes clearer in a varied panorama: see a hill which bears houses, gardens and other things. If each of these objects is seen distinctly, one can measure the expanse of the whole. But when each object does not present a distinct aspect, one becomes incapable to measure detail by detail and thus to know the total size of the hill. And even, objects close to us and very varied on which one takes a general look, without looking at all their details, seem all the smaller since each of them flinched faster from our gazes: *when we see the detail, we can measure them exactly*, and we know *their total size.*" [II, 8, 1]

What preoccupies Plotinus is the *true* size, the *true* distance and – for the purpose of the search of these elements – the presence on the image of *all* the details and the distinct colours (*true*, as well), and as everywhere else, to identify the amount of "real" in the emptiness of matter. Yet, the true size, the true distance, are recognizable only if all the details are present, and none of the colours faded; and this excludes, in turn, the foreshortening and the aerial geometrical perspective. In other words, according to Plotinus each image of an object subjected to a useful contemplation should ideally be fixed in the foreground, and the different elements of a single image should be aligned side by side on one plane.

We will see in a moment that the art of Late Antiquity abandons the good, classical tradition in favour of the two directions Plotinus recommends in his text: willingly giving up depictions of groups of characters and objects placed side by side, and preferring to bring them to the foreground which becomes the sole plane; and in parallel, it is attached meticulously to the representation of the least detail of the costume and hairstyles, weapons, harnesses, accessories; it replaces, finally, the faded and dulled colours of distant things with local tones, flat and unvarying, which are the same for all objects represented. All these processes, according to Plotinus, allow us to better recognize *true* size and *true* colour, that is the *true* characteristics of the figured object.

Plotinus also teaches us that "surface" vision even safeguards us, under certain circumstances, against the perception of matter:

> Depth (βάθος) (of the being or the thing), is matter (ὕλη), and that is why matter is dark (σκοτεινή). The light which illuminates it is the form (λόγος); intelligence too sees the form. Seeing the form in a being, it judges that the depth of this being is a darkness situated under the light; likewise, the luminous eye, carrying its look on the light or the colours which are sort of lights (καὶ χρόας φῶτα ὄντα), discerns the existence of the dark and material background hidden beneath the coloured surface. [II, 4, 5]

It would follow that the image which tries to reflect the Intelligence would have to neglect and even banish the representation of "depth" and of the "dark" (the figuration of space generally leading to the distinction between more or less lit spaces) and to limit itself to the "coloured surface" which is supposedly illuminated in all its parts, and therefore devoid of shadows. This programme finds a systematic realisation in paintings, increasingly numerous, starting from Late Antiquity. Plotinus, who could have seen them – or foreseen this trend in painting – might have acclaimed them as attempts to depict the luminous and chromatic form, image of the Νοῦς.

Other conditions must be filled to make the contemplation of an image efficacious. These conditions are at the same time physical and "mystical":

> [...] the eye must make itself likewise and similar to the seen object in order to contemplate it. Never did an eye see the sun unless it had first become like the sun, and

> never could a soul have vision of Beauty unless it is itself beautiful. Therefore, may every being become first divine and beautiful, if he wants to contemplate God and Beauty. [I, 6, 9]

Then, in another passage, Beauty must be contemplated "with the inner eye" or – the same thought expressed negatively – "not with the eyes of the body".

The importance of this declaration is evident: it implies that one does not see the image in the same way with bodily eyes as with inner eyes – a new and furthermore suggestive observation for historians since one will often find it written by theologians and sermon-writers of the Middle Ages about Christian images. It is not Plotinus, by the way, who first perceived this phenomenon: the idea itself, as well as the expression "inner eyes", date back to the experience of mystery religions which invited the image of the divinity to be contemplated with the eyes of the faithful.[6]

We will later encounter more affinities between the doctrine we are occupied with here and the ideas and practices of mystery religions. It will suffice, for now, to underline this conviction of Plotinus that only the image contemplated with the inner eyes is able to fulfil its supreme function, that is to reveal a reflection of the intelligible.

6 Cf. Plutarch, who, also knowing the practices of mystery cults, declared: on the face of the divine statue, one contemplates the facts revealed by the gods "like we perceive them in a dream". Through the image of Isis, the worshipper sees the goddess herself and his soul "will drink from her inexpressible beauty" (*Isis and Osiris*, ch. 78). Apuleius (*The Metamorphoses*, ch. 24) uses similar terms to describe the sensations of the mystery cultist of Isis contemplating the statue of the goddess in a state of rapture: "He enjoys the inexpressible delight which is emitted by the simulacrum of the divinity".

Yet, it is obvious that such a way of seeing would not leave the artist indifferent: first spectator of his work, and informed of what others after him would be looking for in it, he was tempted to facilitate this search and to reveal in it once and for all not only the appearance of the model like it presented itself to his corporal eyes, but the elements of this superior essence that his work was supposed to reflect, and that his inner eye was supposed to recognise. Practice quickly stabilised a certain amount of methods for this representation of the intelligible (we will see examples), which are as much stereotypical, maybe more, than the usual methods for creating realistic images.

But in principle, and down to works made serially using preconceived formulas, a doctrine like the one of Plotinus could only favour an art of expression and imagination which enlarged the gap between Nature and image. Many works of Late Antiquity belong to this category of works, conceived by artists for beholders who – being invited, one and the other, to contemplate Nature with the inner eyes – tried to interpret the physical appearance of beings and things, in order to make the intelligible appear better. Christian religion favoured this attitude and these attempts.

Plotinus asks himself another question: where exactly does the phenomenon of sight happen? Is it in the eye and the soul of the one who sees, or in the place where the seen object is, and where the light of the eye will reproduce it?

> Sensations are not figures or imprints that occur in the soul [...]; because, according to us, no imprint of the

> perceivable object, which would draw its form, happens in the soul. [...] When we perceive any object by sight, it is clear that we see it remotely and turn our vision towards it. The impression occurs *obviously at the place where the object is*, and [the soul] does not see because it is modelled by the object like wax by a seal. Because it would not have to look outside if it had inside itself the form of the object it sees.[7] [IV, 6, 1]

One cannot ignore the interest of this text for art history. The art of the end of Antiquity and the early Middle Ages often offers examples of a conventional perspective, of two equally curious types: on the one hand, the "reverse" perspective, by which the represented object, or some of its parts, extend or enlarge as the distance between them and the spectator increases; on the other, it is the "radiant" perspective of some strange images which seem to be seen from above and where the foreshortening of all the represented objects converge towards a central point. These two formulas have a story which begins long before Late Antiquity, since their use is known in the archaic arts of Orient, and children, in their drawings, constantly renew their use.

The text of Plotinus shows how the contemporary science of optics could justify such a conception of the image and restore prestige to archaic formulas. Since the phenomenon of sight happens in the contemplated object, the artist attentive to the state of science conceives his image starting from the represented object and not from the point where he stands. In a way, he merges with the object (and we will

7 Emphasis by André Grabar.

see further that by acting like this he obeys a more general assumption that we also find in Plotinus). He sets the aspect of the objects as they should be presented, from the place where the phenomenon of vision is supposed to happen. The part of a table closest to the spectator will thus appear less large than its most distant part; a building will grow larger as it moves away from the beholder. Or, by applying the same principle more systematically, the artist will incorporate himself entirely in the principal object of his image and will portray everything around like a sort of panorama, which he would observe around him if he were merged with the represented object.

It is possible that Late Antiquity returned to these archaic formulas because they corresponded better to the science of the time. This science, at least, was able to explain and justify its use. It could not, however, go as far as to substitute everywhere the reverse and radiant perspective to the normal perspective, familiar to Hellenistic and Roman art by several centuries at that point. The normal perspective thus continued to be used next to the others and two-dimensional images – nothing better characterises the incertitude of artists of this time for everything related to the representation of space. It is obvious that their sensibility, in this regard, had strangely diminished, and therein lies one of the essential phenomena of Late Antique art, which contributed the most to the decline of the classical aesthetic (just like at the end of the Middle Ages, it is the notion of space and volume, rediscovered in the figurative arts, which marks the beginning of a new epoch).

These peculiar hesitations in the representation of space and the third dimension in the works of Late Antiquity (which the Middle Ages will inherit from this period) cannot be wholly explained without involving the more general cause of the deep discredit of ideas related to vision, which were until then traditionally accepted. Here again, there is no better witness and thinker than Plotinus.

For Plotinus, the role of the image – as already mentioned – is to offer a vision of the Νοῦς, *an intellectual vision*. It is in fact only contemplation that can permit, by neglecting pure matter which is non-being, to bring into being the spiritual order that is reflected in matter by forming it. It is this very act of contemplating the Intelligible that creates this order, which makes the perceivable world a reflection of the Νοῦς: "Spiritualist physics", Bréhier observes,[8] opposed to the normal "mechanical physics"; spiritualist physics whose principle is that the parts are not elements of the whole, but productions of the whole (in order to contemplate the Νοῦς, it is introduced into matter). The idea of the whole is therefore more real than its parts.

That is what Plotinus affirms by declaring that "the world becomes transparent to the mind". He summarises in this way, as Bréhier notes,[9] a mental operation described in the *Fifth Ennead*. According to this theory, vision is created by contact between the light within the eye and external light. Plotinus postulates that separation between the two lights is removed, they become transparent to one another and

8 Émile BRÉHIER, *La philosophie de Plotin* (n. 3), pp. 56–57.

9 The rest of this paragraph is borrowed from Émile BRÉHIER, *Notice sur l'Ennéade v*, ch. 8 (n. 5), p. 129.

interpenetrate. At the same time, light is normally stopped and reflected by solid objects. Plotinus supposes that this solidity too is removed, and that in this way the *transparency of objects* becomes absolute: all the objects interpenetrate without limiting themselves and without limiting the light (v, 8, 4, 4–11). He goes further. In visible things, the objects are limiting, mutually interfering with and mixing each other up. But one can suppose that this difficulty and this mix, which only come from the resistance of visible things, are thus removed. One will then have ideas in a pure state: movement that is ceaseless, truly unalterable rest, beauty without blending in of ugliness (v, 8, 4, 11–15). In vision, there is *spatial extent* between the one who sees and the environment where he stands. Plotinus invites us to suppress this exteriority and to suppose the environment absorbed in the being, the being in the environment: *such is the state of intellectual vision.*

Finally, we distinguish between the light and the source from which it emanates (mainly the stars). Let us remove this distinction: may everything be the source of light and may be as well. We will have a vision where it is no longer necessary to distinguish between parts (v, 8, 4, 18–27). And to clarify this thought: "[...] there is no point where one can fix one's own limits in order to say: up to that point it is me." (vi, 5, 7) In other words, the state of contemplation of the Intelligible is not accompanied by self-conscience; rather, all our activity is directed towards the contemplated object: we become this object, we offer ourselves to it like matter that it shapes, we are still ourselves only in potential: to see, one must lose awareness of self, and to have conscience of this vision, one must in some way cease to see. Therefore, if we want to see by being aware of vision, we have to detach from it sufficiently, but not fully in order to be able to come back and return to our discretion. It is in this sort of movement alternating separation and union that the state of absorption of ourselves in the whole – supreme goal of the ideal intellectual contemplation – is born (v, 8, 11, 1–13).

A similar – or identical – method leads to perfect knowledge. "The truth exists for us only in a row of propositions we state about things. Let us postulate a science that directly affects the beings that we state. Then it does not *follow* its object, it *has* it entirely within, it is *identical* to it." (v, 8, 4, 40–56) Now, according to Plotinus (v, 8, 5, 3–4), it is a phenomenon of this kind that art presents, in that it possesses a "wisdom" that "contains the very model it imitates". This wisdom is not made of theorems, but is total; it is a unity, not that it is composed by multiple elements it brings to unity, but rather, starting from this unity, it decomposes into plurality (v, 8, 5).

Plotinus cares a lot about this conception of knowledge – a unique and total knowledge, which is not acquired by successive additions; and he believes it is superior to the other: "[...] the wisdom of the gods and blessed does not express itself through propositions, but through beautiful images." (v, 8, 5) "It is what the Egyptians had understood, writing not with letters forming sounds and sentences, but with signs *of which each is a science*, a wisdom, a real thing *grasped at once*, and not a reasoning or deliberation." (v, 8, 6) The script of the Greco-Romans offers no such thing, but art, as always, possesses this remarkable advantage, in the eyes of Plotinus, to allow this *immediate and total knowledge*. For this knowledge is acquired by the intellectual vision (of which we spoke earlier). This means of knowledge, declared perfect (since it alone leads to the contemplation of the real), "is not thought, but this kind of *contact* or *touch*, ineffable and *unintelligent,* prior to intelligence when it is not born yet, and when there is touching without thought" (v, 3, 10).

Historians of philosophy agree that, as Plotinus wrote, "it is the value of rational knowledge itself which is attained" (Bréhier), and no longer, as Plato and Aristoteles believed, a tool for knowledge, nor was it the starting point of a progressive synthesis (Bréhier); that, in the system of Plotinus, knowledge has transformed into an imprecise emotion, a vital and formless feeling, an elusive "*Stimmung*" (Rudolf Eucken).

In art history, these same theories mark a turning point which is neither less distinct, nor less significant. During Plato's time, and the long period spanning from Phidias to Plotinus, it was not doubted that art objectively imitates material Nature, either by putting the emphasis on the laws of harmony which reveal instinct and science, or by trying to render the appearance of things as they are perceived by the eye. One has, like Plato, given preference to the first method, or – like others – to the second. But these varying preferences did not rattle the general attitude of Antiquity towards art, which had the mission of imitating things and beings of the perceivable world. Thus, the Greco-Roman aesthetic and forms of Antique art – Greek, then Roman – could keep their full authority, throughout the centuries.

But this art could no longer offer its methods and expressive formulas (or at least its methods and forms were not sufficient anymore) to those who, like Plotinus, asked the artwork to be not an imitation of material Nature (regardless if immediate or idealised imitation), but the starting point for a metaphysical experience, a way of creating an ineffable contact with the Νοῦς, which the artwork is supposed to reflect. Whilst every image of Greek tradition, classical or Hellenistic, stabilises the results of a rational analysis of the figured object, Plotinus recognises in art, conceived in view of his contemplation of the Intelligible, the expression of an immediate and total knowledge of things, of the universal soul. Objective art supposes a beholder who, whilst contemplating, never ceases to be conscious of either the vision or himself, as two distinct entities; in contrast, the intellectual vision of Plotinus allows an absorption of the beholder into the vision and into the whole, or more accurately, a curious alternation at brief intervals, separations and unions of the spectator and the vision – in a state of half-consciousness which alone, according to Plotinus, can lead to a metaphysically useful contemplation. For rational knowledge, just as for art which strives to imitate Nature and relies on the analyses of the data of our senses, distinguishing a plurality of facts that are linked together is indispensable, because it alone allows recognition in the imitative image of the object or the objects that wanted to be imitated. It will be the more perfect, for example, if it is possible to distinguish with precision the relative size of the objects, the volume of each of them, the distance between them. Yet, in Plotinus' experience, perfect vision is "transparent", as he says, meaning a vision where the objects are neither autonomous nor impenetrable, where space will be absorbed, where light will cross solid bodies without problem and where the beholder himself will not be able to discern the limits which separate him from the contemplated object.

A programme of this type could not have been achieved, even partially, by means of classical and Hellenistic Greek art, nor, especially, by ancient Roman art. Something else was needed. Examination of Late Antique works, in particular monuments of the Late Empire, pagan and particularly Christian, allows us to observe methods and forms unknown to the Greek and Roman artists of yore, which seem to respond to preoccupations such as those of Plotinus. In contrast to the principles and methods of anterior artists, the way in which those images, reliefs, and statues were conceived in their whole or in some of their elements, could have facilitated the kind of contemplation recommended by Plotinus.

I limit myself to indicating some of the artistic elements which can be brought in relation to the different points of the doctrine of Plotinus, by referring for the detail of the interpretation, as was proposed for each of the artworks which will serve as examples, to the iconographic dossier.

A) The image is brought to a single plane, in painting and in flat relief [FIGS 3 AND 7]: this tendency corresponds to the postulate of the vision of *true* size, of *true* colour, in short of *true* Nature, an indispensable condition to move closer to the contemplation of the "real". The light is equal and diffuse; projected shadows are absent; the other shadows fade and neutralise as if there were multiple sources of light.

B) Details of the represented object (hairstyles, costumes, fabrics with their ornaments, weapons with their decoration) [FIGS 5, 6, AND 9] are reproduced with extreme care, which might even hamper the overall effect: another tendency which corresponds to a condition for the contemplation of the "real".

C) Reverse perspective (the object or the objects represented grow larger or increase in proportion to the distance of the beholder) [FIGS 1, 7 AND 8] and radiant perspective (the depicted objects radiate in all directions from a central point) [FIG. 2]: formulas which constitute attempts to set the observer in the object he beholds. In fact, the normal aspect of things could be re-established by imagining the beholder standing in the middle of the painting or the relief.

D) Characters and objects unfold on a surface parallel to the picture or relief; but this surface is nothing but an ideal plane since the characters on it can cover each other partially (for example, laying their feet on those of their neighbours) and interpenetrate, without touching each other, enter in contact with the ground or with furniture, without joining to it, or, with the same ease, stay suspended in air [FIGS 6 AND 13]. Out of habit (but not always), one applies a certain formation to the representation of beings and things, which formerly gave the illusion of a plastic form specific to them; but the processes of doing so are reproduced with such errors that an atrophy of the performers' awareness for plasticity must be supposed: especially the imitations of models of classical style reveal this weakening of perception for stereometric forms [FIGS 1, 3, 6, 7, AND 8]. Yet, all these elements which make the body into a thing without volume, without weight, and seem to take it away from the normal order that rules the perceivable world, lead us towards a vision of this world made "transparent", as Plotinus puts it.

E) A cloud of light that envelops a character [FIG. 1]. This is a special case of the same pursuit – the very type of innovations from artists of the Late Empire: the luminous sphere, though surrounding the figure, has no volume; it is of an absolute transparency (it lets objects appear which it should conceal), and although we perceive only the subtle edge of its geometrically regular outline, its presence is manifest in the luminosity it confers to the figure it enshrouds. As it happens, these are depictions of theophanies, and that is why such "transparent" images, that is to say devoid of the characteristics of matter, deserve above all to be related closely to the visions of the Plotinian Νοῦς.

F) Images where Nature is subjected to regular geometrical schemes; compositions where figures and objects assimilated to ornamental motives participate in a rhythmical motion, by repeating the same stereotypical movement [FIGS 2, 7, 8, AND 13]. The artist lays out as he intends the figures of Nature and, at his discretion, introduces order and homogeneity where, according to the expression of Plotinus, there was "mixing" and disorder (this is also valid for portraits: cf. FIGS 4 AND 5). He ensures unity where matter was offering the spectacle of plurality, and, by acting in this way, creates images which come closer to the vision of the Intelligible. He also justifies Plotinus by proclaiming the "wisdom of art". In fact, conceived as such, this art renders clear the reason behind this wisdom, namely that it contained in itself the model it imitated, and was therefore able to offer the beholder the direct science of the Intelligible. The movement, alternating rhythmical compositions, also contributed to creating the state of half-consciousness that Plotinus believed was favourable to this type of knowledge, close to revelation.

Most artworks that I will use as examples of this aesthetic researches date from the fourth, fifth, and sixth centuries. One relief, in which the portrait of Plotinus has sometimes been recognised [FIG. 11] and belongs to the same era as the philosopher, can be dated around 270 and figures among the most ancient manifestations of the new tendencies of ancient art in its decline. It is in the third century indeed, but especially in the following centuries, that the originality of what we might call the art of Late Antiquity (*Spätantike*) asserts itself, and, from Constantine up to the first heirs of Justinian, we can observe a multiplication of the examples of methods and forms that we believe can be linked to the ideas of Plotinus.

However, by speaking of their apparition in the third century and their generalised acceptation from the fourth century, we think only of the work stemming from Greek and Latin countries. In the Levant, in Egypt and in Syria, in the half-Greek, half-local art practised there, we know works of analogue tendency since the beginning of our era, at the latest. The Egyptian funerary paintings of the imperial period, and especially the reliefs and frescoes of the sanctuaries and hypogea of Palmyra and Dura (the reliefs of the temple of Bel in Palmyra [FIG. 12] date from the reign of Augustus, the other monuments belong to the second and third centuries[10]), already employ the image brought to a single plane, the flat depiction of figures and objects, without volume or weight, the meticulously exact representations of the details of certain objects (hairstyles, costumes, furniture, accessories, embroidered textiles, etc.) opposed to the geometrical schematising of the characters or landscape; and finally, the ornamental and geometrical interpretations of objects and human beings – in short most of the committed positions which would make the works of Greco-Latin Late Antiquity innovative.

We do not deal here with the more remote origins of these artistic processes, which as a matter of fact have not been fully elucidated. The earlier art of Mesopotamia and Egypt has a role in this, and among the archaisms that it bequeathed to Levantine artists of the Roman period, we must cite the important yet rare method of the radiant perspective. But all the original features that the late works, Syrian and Egyptian, have in common with the Greco-Latin monuments of Late Antiquity are not explained by the rebirth of local tradition in the Near East. The frontality of characters, in particular, an essential and extremely frequent trait of these

10 Best reproductions of the reliefs of Palmyra: Henri SEYRIG, "Antiquités syriennes", *Syria*, XV (1934), PL. XVIII ff. Paintings and reliefs at Dura: Franz CUMONT, *Fouilles de Doura-Europos* (1922–1923), Paris 1926, Atlas, PL. XXXI–LX; Michael ROSTOVTZEFF, *Dura-Europos and its Art*, Oxford 1938, PL. XIII–XV, XVII, XVIII, XX–XXIV; *idem*, "Dura and the Problem of Parthian Art", *Yale Classical Studies*, V (1935), FIGS 71–73, 76, 77, 79; Robert DU MESNIL DU BUISSON, *Les peintures de la synagogue de Doura-Europos*, Vatican City 1939, PL. VIII ff.

two series of works, does not belong to either of those traditions and instead recalls the frontal figures of archaic Greek art. Attempts at imitating archaic-style sculptures were by the way frequent in the imperial period. But it might be more useful, thinking about Syrian (and partly Egyptian) paintings and reliefs, generally made for religious and funerary purposes, to evoke on the one hand the renewed success at this period of the *xoana* and other archaic and rustic depictions of the gods. On the other hand, to evoke the importance, in the Levant, of mystery religions, which favoured the direct communication of the believer with the divinity by means of contemplation, either of its cult-image or through miraculous apparition. These contemplations, useful to salvation, frequent and sought by every believer during his terrestrial career, would happen again at the moment of his ascension towards the divinity, after death.[11]

In short, in the art destined to the living and in funerary imagery, for representations of the gods and of believers (the two partners of these contemplations), the frontal representation, which corresponded to the "eye-to-eye" contemplation of the divinity, and, consequently, of the Intelligible, had chances to establish itself in art even outside of the themes for which it had originally been created: the prestige of the frontal attitude and the frequency of such images would

11 The frontal depictions of the emperors, which emerge in the third century and establish themselves definitively at the beginning of the fourth century, belong to the same type of idea: these figures represent the sacred sovereign as he reveals himself, a divinity, to mere mortals who place themselves at his feet, during the official receptions at the Palace. – We study more extensively the problem of the influence of these religious elements on the imagery of Late Antiquity in our book: *Martyrium. Rercherches sur le culte des reliques et l'art à la fin de l'Antiquité*, 2 vols, Paris 1946.

have made it a favoured formula of the art of Late Antiquity and of the early Middle Ages. This assumption relative to the origins of the frontal figure in Syrian (and Egyptian) art first, and in all Mediterranean countries after, is incidentally closely linked to the problem of the connections between the ideas of Plotinus and their sculptural analogues, in third- and fourth-century works.

Franz Cumont was able to show that Plotinus had a personal experience of the mystery religions of his time, that of Isis-Osiris probably, and that his descriptions of the contemplation of the Intelligible take as a starting point the practice of the one-on-one contemplation, by the neophyte on the way to his consecration, of the mysterious effigy of the divinity, at the heart of its sanctuary:[12] "To contemplate this god, one must commune with oneself, like within a temple, and remain silent beyond all things of this world, as one would consider statues [...] especially that which shines first" (the adyton of the temple) (v, 1, 6).

Elsewhere, he writes about this contemplation in the *cella* of the temple: "The vision gained inside [the sanctuary] and the intimate union made not with the statue, but with the divinity herself [...], contemplation [which] is not a spectacle, but another form of vision, the ecstasy." (vi, 9, 11) Finally, regarding the ceremonies where one contemplated the statues of the gods, Plotinus observed that their divinity appeared only to those of the acolytes who did not look at them with their bodily eyes.[13] Thanks to other texts that speak about

12 Franz Cumont, "Le culte égyptien et le mysticisme de Plotin", *Monuments et mémoires de la Fondation Eugène Piot*, xxv (1921), pp. 77–92.

13 Cf. *supra*, pp. 67–68.

similar visions, either in front of images of the gods, or during miraculous apparitions, we find analogies with the Plotinian visions: the epopt is often in a state of semi-consciousness ("neither awake nor asleep"), his soul overflows with inexpressible delight, the vision shines of a wonderful light; directed towards him, the divinity of the theophany fixes him with its gaze. And if it is the believer in front of his god, his reason is filled by the clarity emanating from it so that, by way of the vision, he becomes equal to the god and confuses himself with him:[14] crucial analogy for the absorption of the Intelligible by the beholder, within the object he contemplates, in Plotinus' work.

In short, although as I just recalled, the philosopher had to draw from his memories of mystical contemplations by the adepts of Isis, and other analogous practices of theophanies, to describe the contemplation of the Intelligible, these writings can in turn help us to interpret the works of art which seem to call upon or reflect mystical experiences comparable to his own. It is in this way that the testimony of Plotinus is substantiating the hypothesis we have just summarised regarding the origins of the frontal characters in the art of Late Antiquity: the doctrines of Plotinus on the intelligent vision offer us, by a sort of backwards motion, a way to recognise at the hands of the creators of some particular representations, like the character in frontal attitude, ideological intentions which would otherwise risk escaping our notice. By generalising, through Plotinus' work, as well, we notice the probable ideological origins of other processes and forms foreign to the earlier Greek tradition, which we have noted from the art

14 I gather the evidence of the ancients on these visions in my book *Martyrium* (n. 11).

of the Late Antiquity. For a long time, we have seen in this nothing but the signs of the decadence of ancient art; and although we are now often inclined to attribute its origins to the Orient, it is without explaining in a satisfying manner the reasons for which these Eastern influences could find enough credit in the West to undermine the several centuries-old Greek artistic tradition, and substitute more rudimentary formulas to its aesthetics.

Yet, research on the imperial period, which tended to make art an instrument capable of adapting to the predominant ideological and religious preoccupations, could provide the key to many peculiarities of the works of Late Antiquity, and notably those which respond to the doctrine of Plotinus on the vision of the Intelligible. Such research, on the work of artists of this time, could reveal that they borrowed from the arts of Syria and Egypt, the origin of mystery religions and religious philosophies that spread towards the West, because they gave to these exotic imports the authority which they shared with the mystical and ideological movements they served. Nevertheless, since, in a current of adaptation of this type, the Eastern imports were not appreciated for themselves, the art of Late Antiquity could have used other sources simultaneously and also turn, as it had, towards the archaic Greek arts, which the ideological and religious experiences of the time favoured much the same as it did the exoticism of the Orient.

It goes without saying that the ideas of Plotinus exerted absolutely *no influence* on the activity of the artists of his time and of the following epoch. A style peculiar to the sculpture in the time of Gallienus which has been thought to have been inspired if not by the philosopher himself, at least by his circle during the last part of his life,[15] has absolutely no relationship with the doctrine we have been occupied with, and with this new art of Late Antiquity. As for the influence of the disciples of Plotinus, we know that in Rome, in the fourth century, the Neoplatonists positioned themselves as champions of the classical tradition in art and that, retrograde in this domain which was too closely tied to their efforts to revive paganism, they encouraged the pastiche of past artworks. That is how, during the ephemeral triumph of the pagan party in Rome, at the end of the fourth century, the few artworks commissioned by the Symmachi and Nicomachi, who had Neoplatonist advisers, stand out through a classical style inspired by the monuments of the times of Augustus or Hadrian[16] [FIG. 14].

However, it is especially (but not exclusively) in the Christian works of Late Antiquity that the new tendencies of art, which find such precious ideological commentary in Plotinus, are manifested. The Neoplatonists hostile to Christianity had certainly not noticed the possible link to establish between the ideas of their master and the artistic works that served the cause of their enemies. This relationship is valuable, obviously, only when we need to contemplate the facts of this epoch looking back several centuries, and for lack of direct declarations by the Christians themselves about the religious value of the artistic forms they used. But in the

15 RODENWALDT, *The Transition* (n. 2); *idem*, "Zur Kunstgeschichte der Jahre 220–270", in *Jahrbuch des deutschen Archäologischen Instituts*, LI (1936), p. 82 ff.

16 Andreas ALFÖLDI, *A Festival of Isis under the Christian Emperors of the IVth Century*, Budapest 1937 (*Dissertationes Pannonicae*, ser. II, fasc. 7), p. 36 ff., 39–40. Cf. Joseph BIDEZ, *Vie de Porphyre*, Gand 1913, p. 70.

absence of such, the testimony of Plotinus seems to me essential to art history. He gives us the outline of an ideological explanation of the research that artists, empirically, had started in his times and that carried on mainly in Christian workshops, during the last centuries of Antiquity. The new aesthetic which would emerge from this research would in the end serve Christian art exclusively. But in the times of Plotinus and even later, analogous artworks could emerge in environments guided by different doctrines.[17]

17 Émile Bréhier was so kind as to read the manuscript of the present study and provide me with precious advice. I ask him to accept my gratitude. I thank Paul Étard for his friendly help.

ILLUSTRATIONS WITH THEIR COMMENTARIES

FIG. 1

Mosaic in Santa Maria Maggiore, Rome (Theophany to Abraham). – First known example of an image of a luminous halo which envelops the whole figure. Here, it is the central character of the theophany to Abraham. Observe the way in which the painter tried to show the transparency of this cloud of light through which neighbouring figures are partially visible. The character of the vision seems to be enclosed in an egg-shaped and geometrically regular space of light which subtracts him from the perceivable world, which itself is immaterial, transparent and colourless: attempt to represent the intelligible. – The table appears in reversed perspective: the side farthest from the beholder is the largest.

Theophany to Abraham
Mosaic, left wall of the nave,
Santa Maria Maggiore, Rome, 432–438

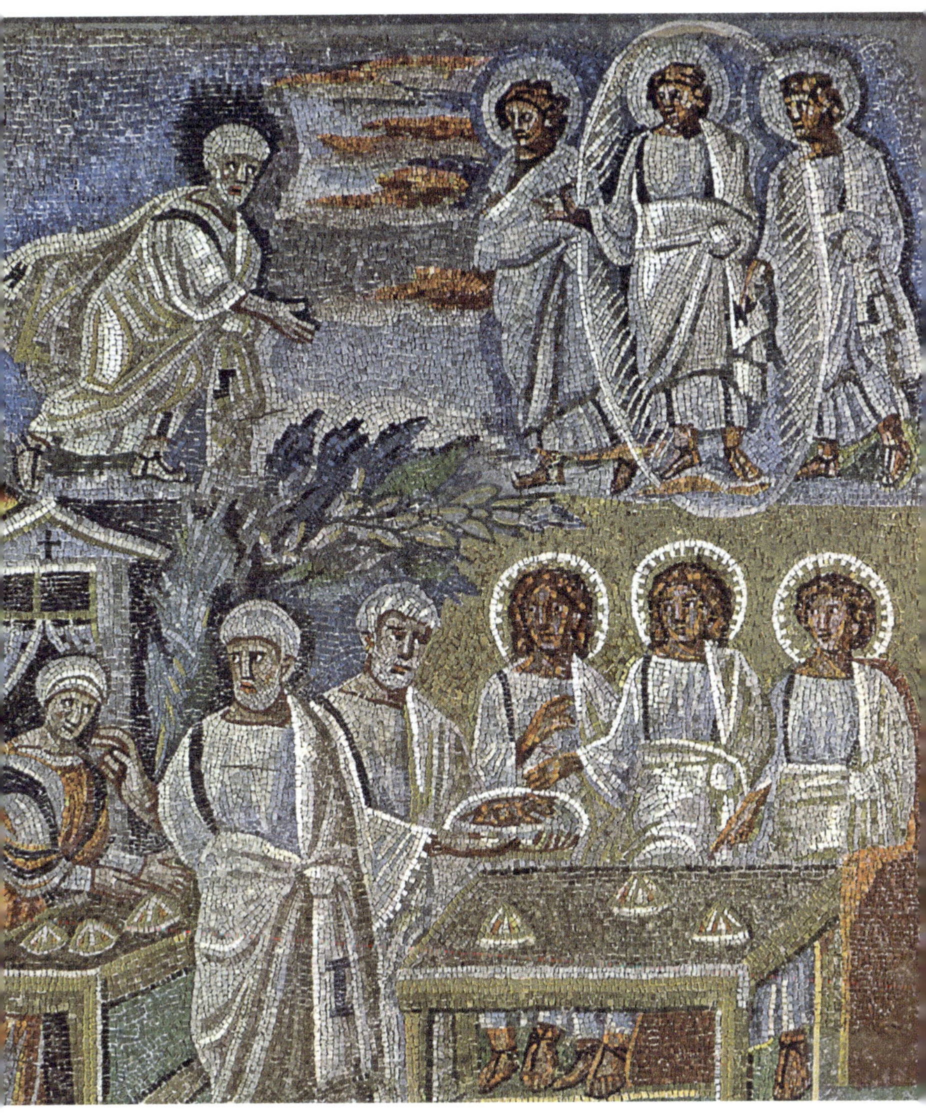

FIG. 2

Illumination of the Cosmas Indicopleustes of the Vatican Library. – Reproduction of the ninth century after an original made in Alexandria in the sixth century: David plays from the Psalm book in presence of his son Solomon. The prophet Samuel is represented in a medallion. Two dancers and six choirs accompany the musician king with their dances and singing. Example of radiant perspective to represent the singers of each choir sitting in a circle. Example also of the simultaneous and contradictory use of two perspectives in one image. In a less striking form, hesitations of this type are frequent in the art of Late Antiquity, and of the Middle Ages.

Choirs of King David
Miniature illumination from Cosmas Indicopleustes,
Christian Topography, ninth century, Constantinople (?)
/ Biblioteca Apostolica Vaticana, Vatican, Vat. Gr. 0699, FOL. 63V

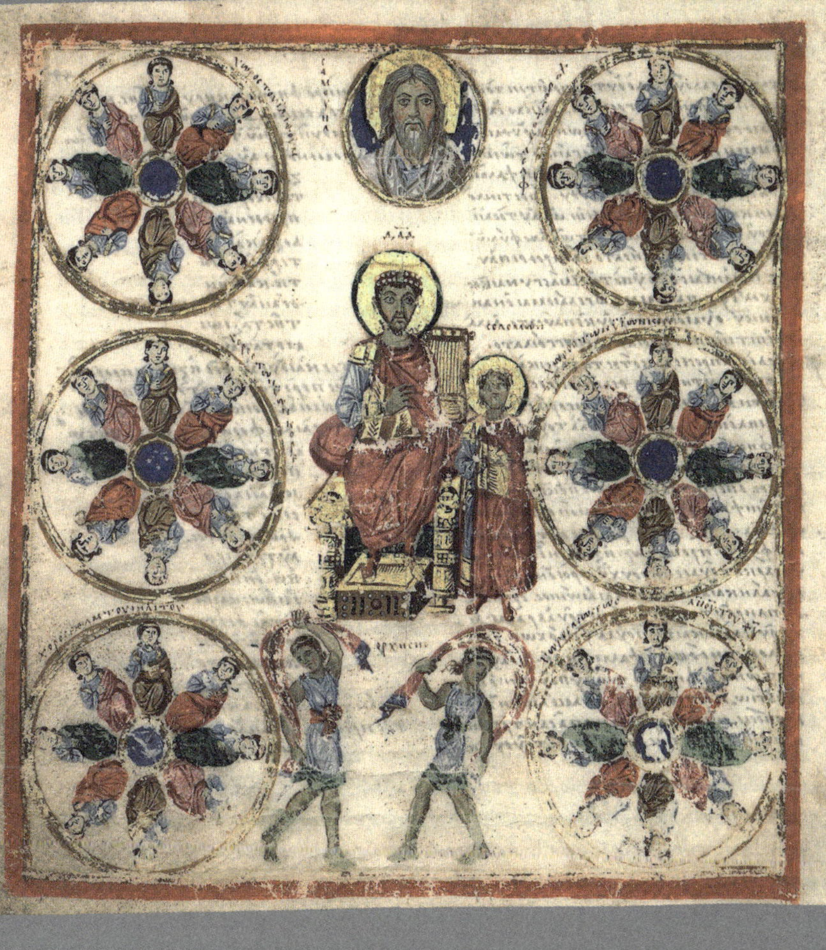

FIG. 3

Mosaic of Sant'Apollinare in Classe in Ravenna. – Sixth century. Scene of a triple sacrifice to God: of Melchizedek offering the bread, of Abel presenting a lamb, of Abraham brining Isaac. All the characters and the table are brought to the first plane; the artifice is specifically striking for the table which, despite the foreshortening of its right side, is projected entirely on the single plane of the image and thus finds itself devoid of all volume. The heads of all characters are represented frontally. The draperies, despite the drawing of the folds which imitate antique models, have no plastic value.

Melchizedech, Abel and Abraham sacrificing on an altar
Mosaic, Sant'Apollinare in Classe, Ravenna, ca 668–685

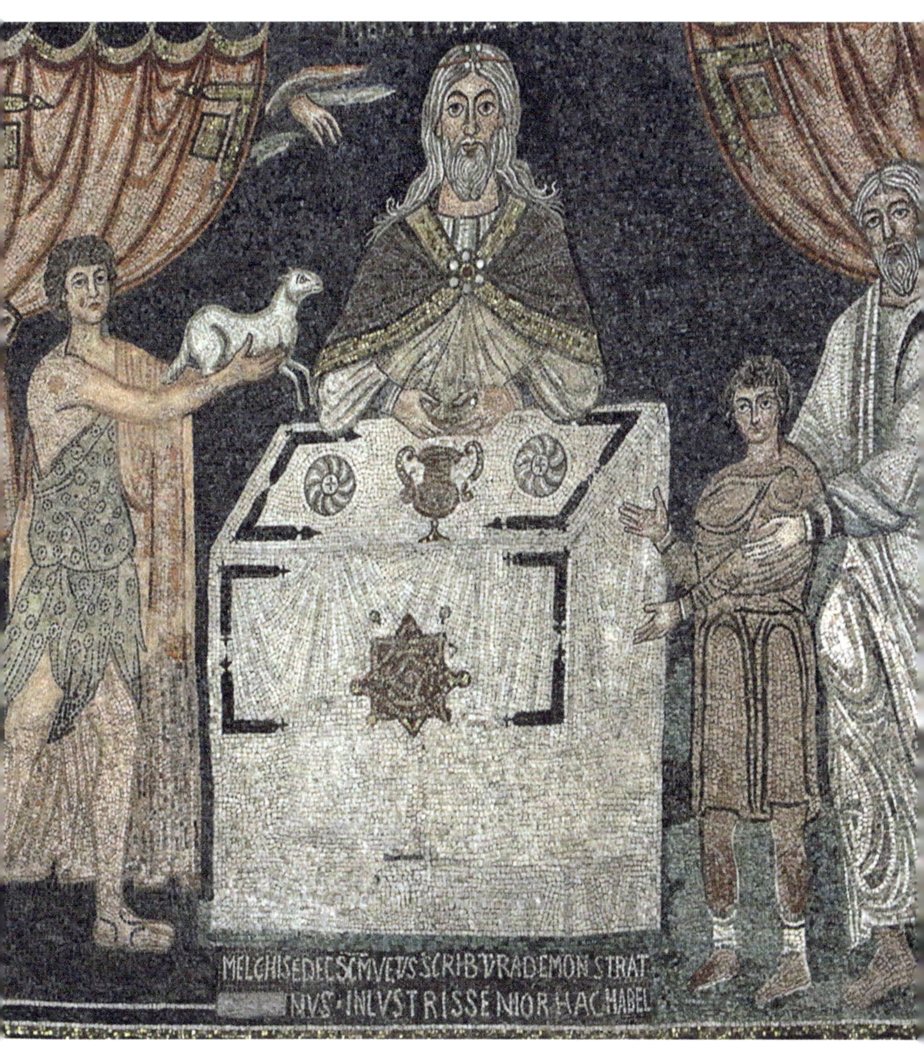
MELCHISEDEC SCMVETVS SCRIB VRADEMON STRAT
NVS · INLVSTRISSENIOR HAC HABEL

FIG. 4

Marble head of an unknown individual. – National Museum in Vienna. Fifth century. Example of a portrait that reunites the precise observation of some details, which seems sketched from life (mouth, wrinkles in the cheeks, opening of the eyes) and a deliberate schematising of the whole: strictly frontal symmetry, almost exaggerated elongation of the head, methodical arrangement of the hair, notably around the mouth. Instead of imitating the physical appearance in all these elements, only a few elements are pointed out (just as for the motives of FIG. 6) which are necessary for the contemplation of the "real" in the model, and one then tries to give "total" knowledge, in other words to capture the *result* of an "Intelligible" vision.

Anonymous male bust, called Eutropios
Marble, half of the fifth century, Ephesos (?)
/ Kunsthistorisches Museum, Antikensammlung, Vienna, Inv. № I 880

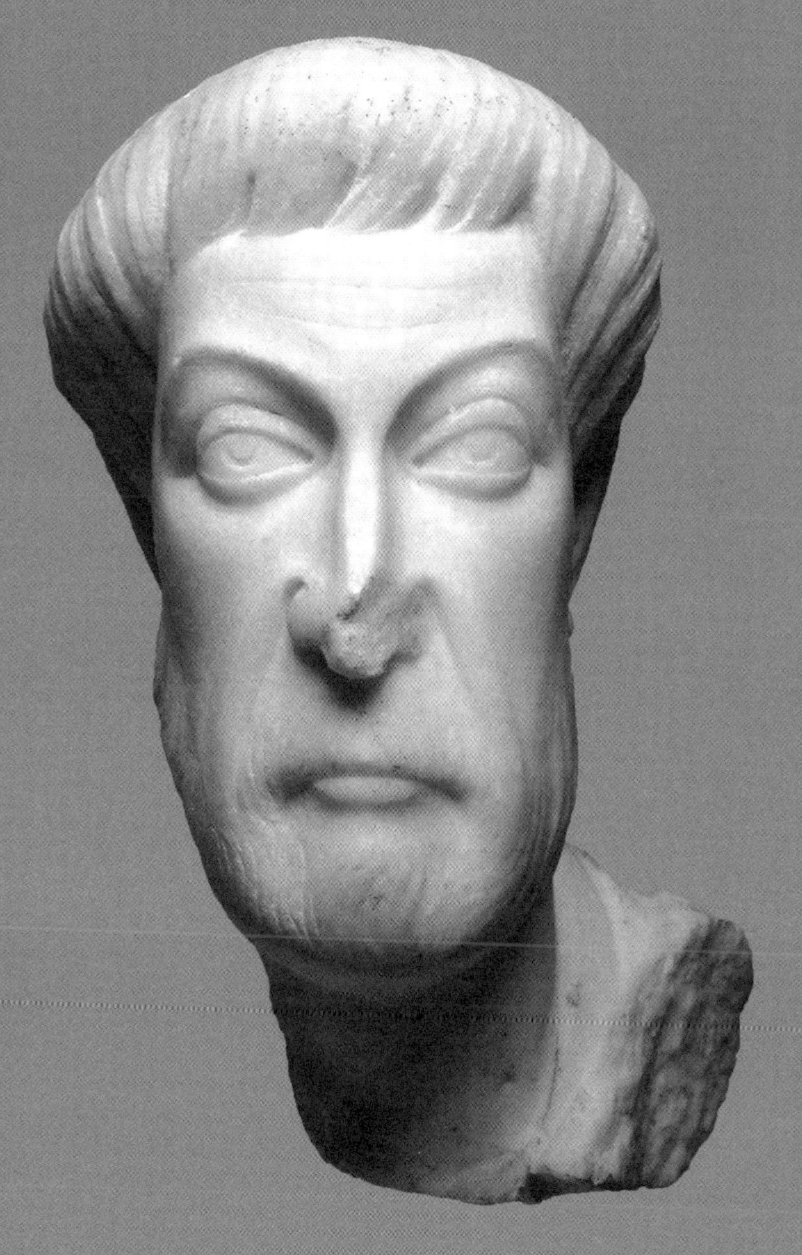

FIG. 5

Head of a bronze statue of an emperor of the fourth century, in Barletta. – Same characteristics as FIG. 4: another attempt at representing not the physical data of the model subjected to the gaze, but the result of contemplation which would be aimed at identifying, with the eyes of the spirit, the deep essence of the depicted individual. See, in the third and fourth century, the substitution of the consumed triumph of a warrior or hunter with that of his dramatic struggle against a foe or wild animal (Rodenwaldt).

Colossal bronze statue of an emperor
Second half of the fifth century, Constantinople (?)
/ Barletta, Apulia

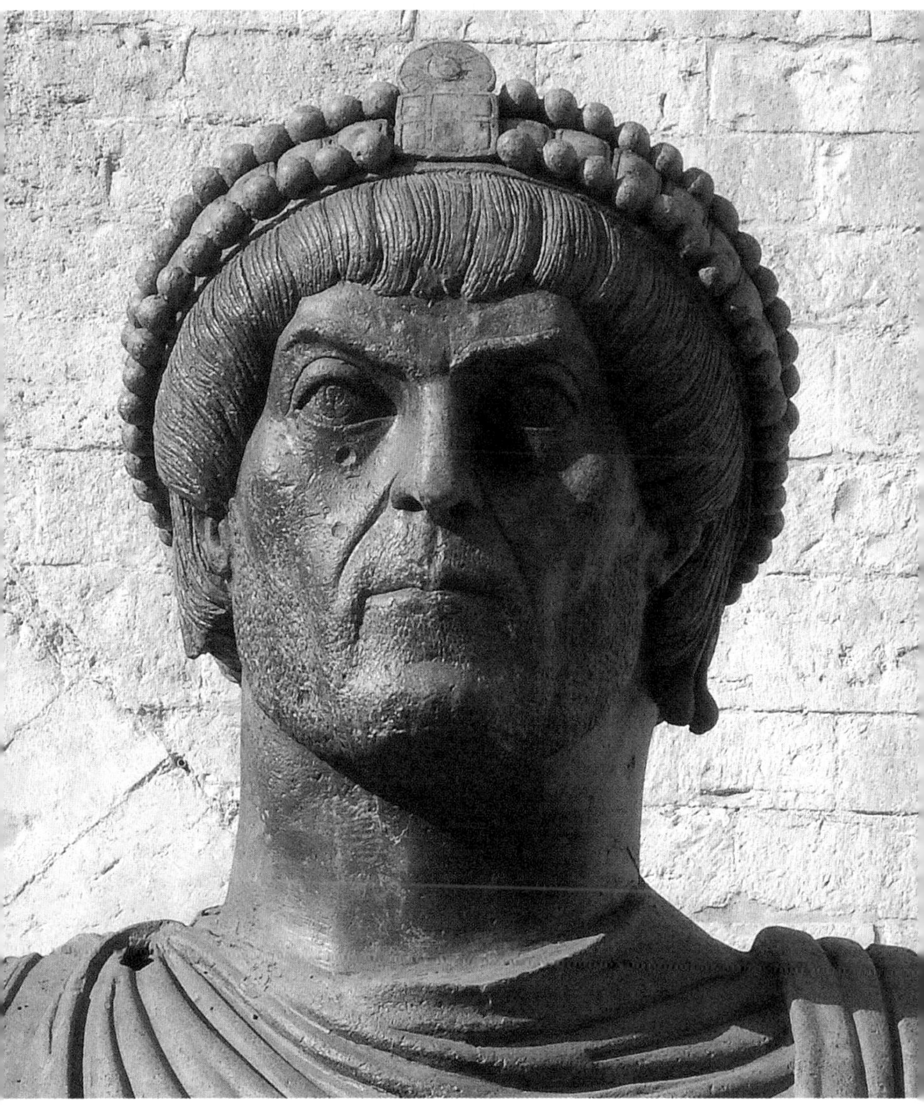

FIG. 6

Silver plate at the Academy of History in Madrid. – Around 400. Detail of a scene depicting an investiture by Theodosius I: two bodyguards. Examples of the meticulous precision given to the representation of the details of weapons, costumes with their ornaments, coiffures, furniture: essential details for the "intelligible" vision of all these objects. Example also of a scene set on a single, abstract plane: the first warrior walks on the base of a column without really leaning on it; the position of the second in relation to the column remains indeterminate: his legs are not represented; same imprecision regarding the position of the throne in relation to the *suppedaneum.*

Missorium of Theodosius I
Silver plate, ca 388–390, Constantinople (?)
/ Real Academia de la Historia, Madrid

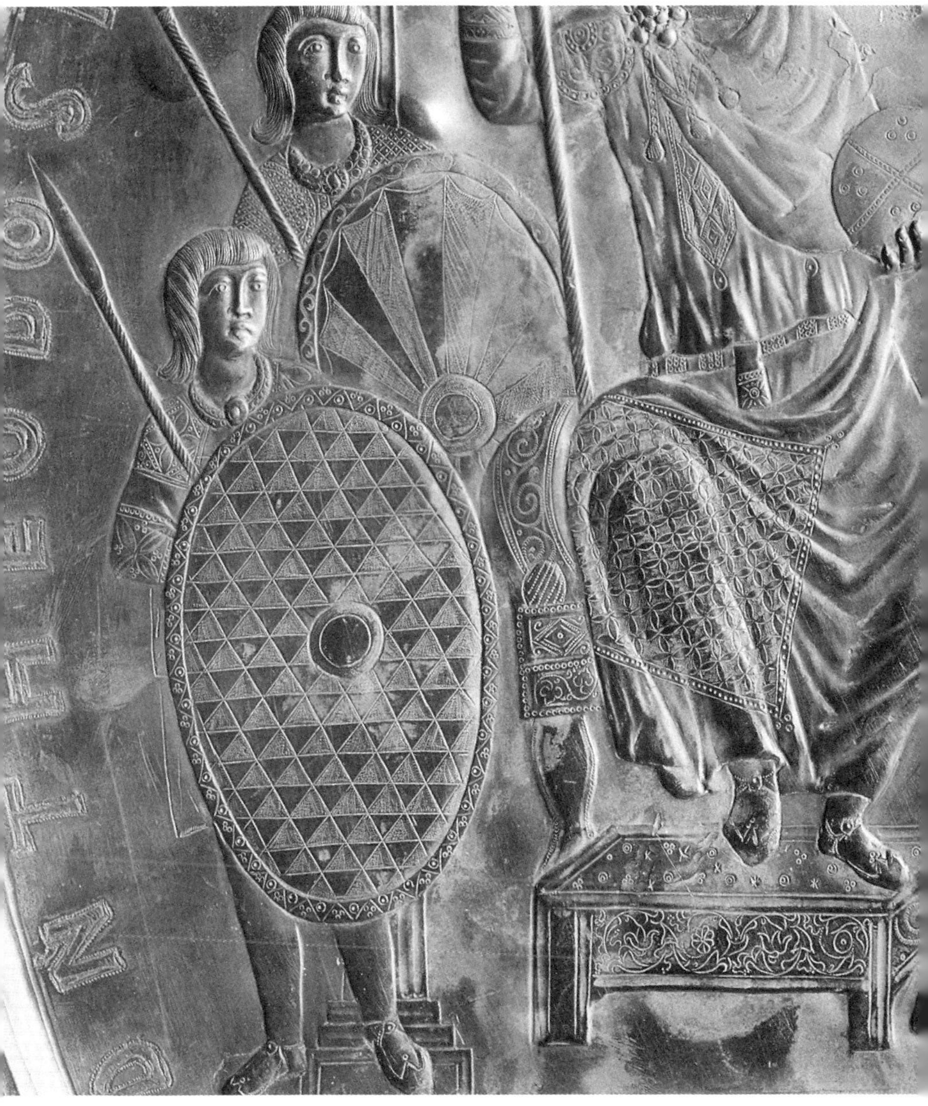

FIG. 7

Ivory plaque at the museum of Dijon, fifth century. – Reunion of Christ and the apostles. Example of reverse perspective: the size of the characters increases from the bottom up. Example of the difficulties experienced by the artist placed in front of a model once created in the frame of the antique perspective and where all the characters were represented around a table which bears a box holding rolled phylacteries of the eight books of Scripture (four books of the prophets and four gospels). The copyist, who is no longer able to represent space in elusive perspective, places four of the twelve apostles in the foreground (see the feet of their four chairs) and arbitrarily attributes the table with its manuscripts and the curtain at the top of the image to the same ideal plane. He confusedly places on the same plane all the other characters, by reattaching them to a sort of semi-circular *suppedaneum*, which is transformed in his view into a vertically placed arch. The figures of the apostles and of Christ expand according to the rays which come from the bottom of the composition. One detail demonstrates that the whole composition, including the apostles around Christ, is projected on a single plane: the curtain hanging from the upper frame of the image comes down, on the right, *behind* the head of an apostle.

Christ amongst Apostles
Ivory, fifth century, North Italy (?)
/ Musée des Beaux-Arts, Dijon, Inv. № CAT 326

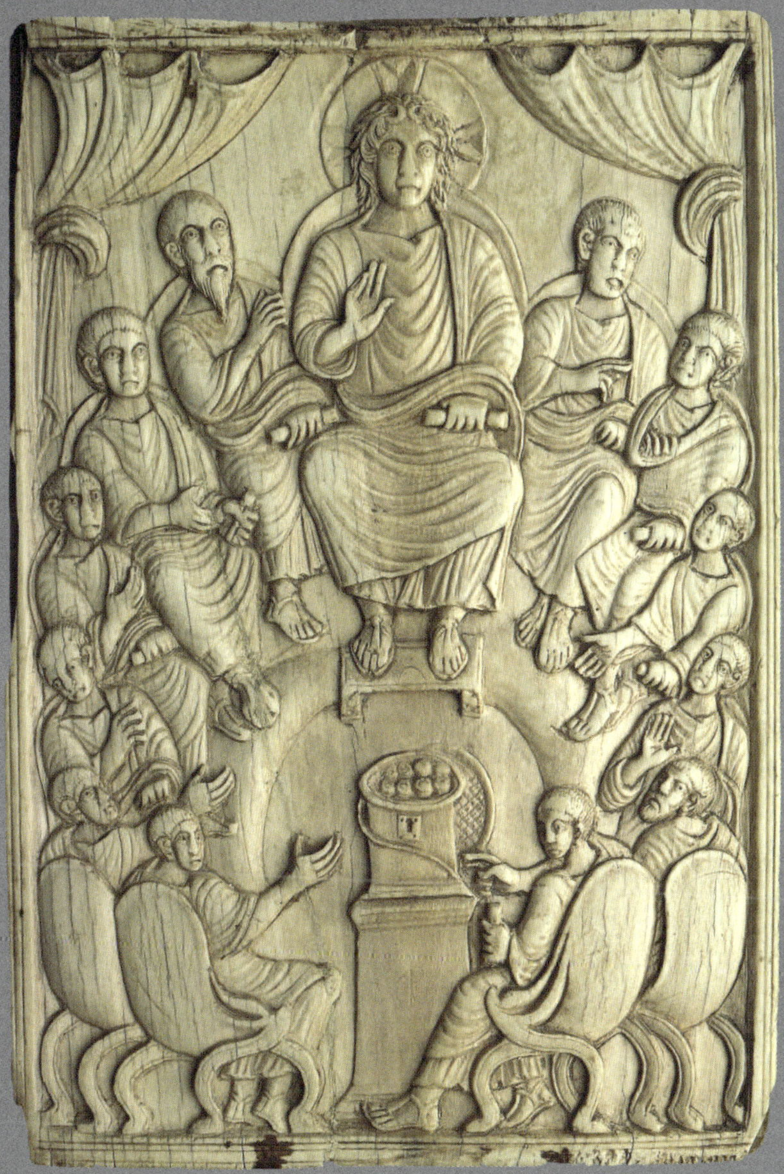

FIG. 8

Relief on the base of the obelisk of Theodosius, in the Hippodrome of Constantinople. – The emperor presides at the games. Around 400. Example of a relief where the real plastic form of beings and objects and their relation in space is not reflected by the artist: the heads of all characters have a more pronounced relief than the rest; the two characters standing under the throne of the sovereign protrude only weakly and flatly, and seem crushed against the balustrade; they do not stand straight; the heads of the characters, overlaid like the steps of the central staircase, all have as much relief, although each one is necessarily distanced from the others. In other words, these are representations which neglect space, volume, and the weight of depicted objects. – Examples of reverse perspective: on the three image zones, it is the bottom one which offers the smallest representations, and the one above which portrays them at the highest scale. In other words, we are invited to watch the scene as though through the gaze of a spectator in the lodge of the emperor.

Obelisk base of Theodosius on the Hippodrome
Marble, 390–392, Constantinople

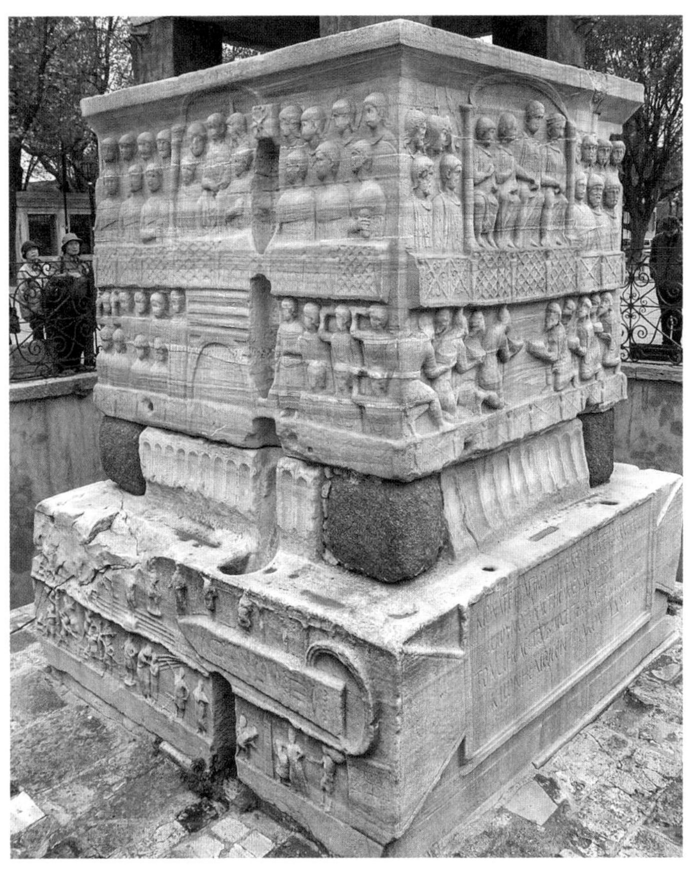

FIG. 9

The tetrarchs. – Porphyry group leaning against the external wall of San Marco in Venice. Around 300. The sculptor, placed in front of the motive of the antique iconography representing two emperors giving each other the accolade, experiences major difficulties: the characters each unfold in a unique and special plane, 90 degrees from each other; only the arm of the left figure timidly tries to reunite them. The archaic stiffness of the characters is striking, as well as the stereotypical representation of their legs, the gesture of their left hands clamping onto the sword handle, the hairstyles, armours, draperies and even the expression of the faces. Opposition between the general schematising of these effigies and the meticulous representation of the armour and the weapons. On the one hand, it is a striking example of the decline of the notion of space (in statuary, a theme like the one of the accolade could not be arbitrarily brought to a single plane, as would have been attempted in a painting of a relief), and of the tendency to give to a dramatic scene the appearance of a composition subject to rigorous order, with symmetric repetition of the same motives and schematic interpretation of all essential components of the work.

Group of Tetrarchs
Porphyry, fourth century, Constantinople / Façade of the treasury of San Marco, south-eastern corner, Venice

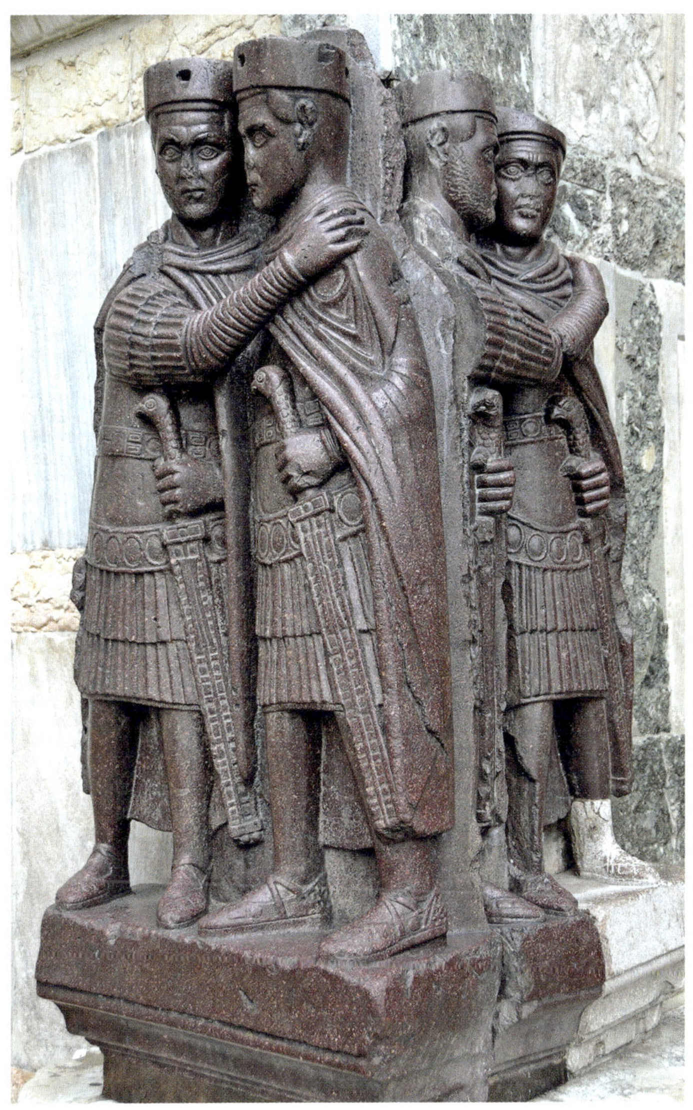

FIG. 10

Porphyry torso of the fifth century, archiepiscopal palace of Ravenna. – Example of a rhythmical interpretation of a statue of a draped character: rigorously frontal attitude, figure unfolded on a single plane and slightly flattened; array of folds of a drawing where long straight lines dominate; arbitrary plastic of the fabric, where folds which are less sculpted than engraved flank others protruding too sharply.

Torso of a figure wearing a chlamys
Porphyry, fifth century (?), Ravenna (?)
/ Archepiscopal Palace, Ravenna

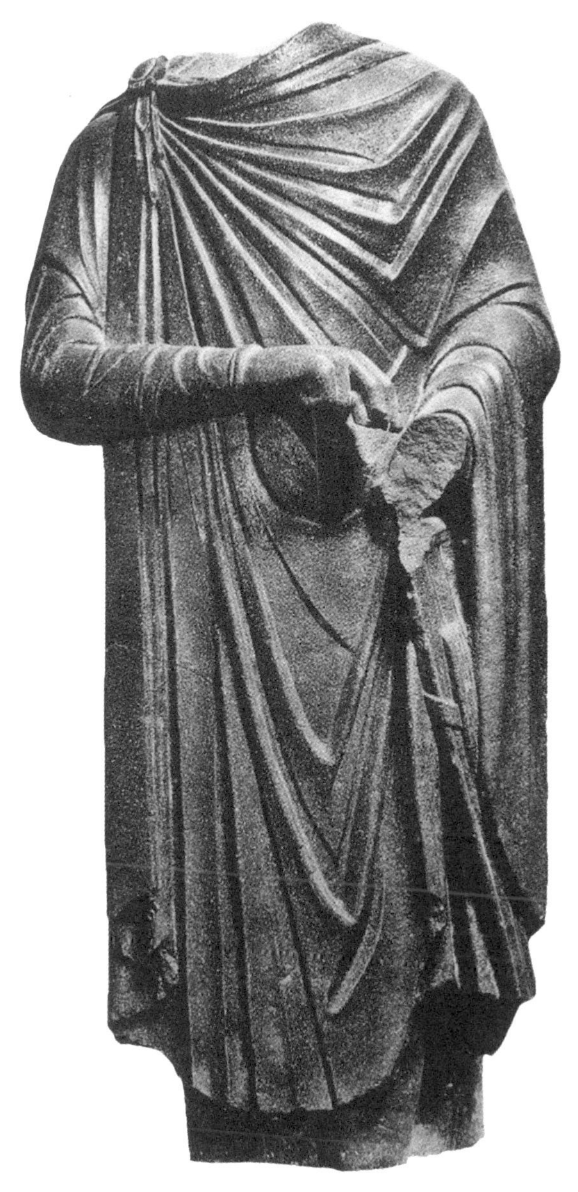

FIG. 11

Façade of a pagan sarcophagus of Villa Torlonia in Rome. – Philosopher, two personifications and three disciples. Around 270. According to Rodenwaldt, the central character depicts Plotinus. Whilst almost everywhere the relief offers a traditional interpretation of figures, of their movements and draperies, one can observe the hesitations of the sculptor in his way of handling the inferior part of the figure of the philosopher sitting frontally. Although this part of the sculpture has little protruding and occurs almost entirely on a single plane, the foreshortening effect of the legs is attained, with great difficulty, by the complicated drawing of draperies thrown on and between the legs of the character. The sculptor, who is not very sensitive anymore to plastic values, thus replaces the methods specific to high relief by those of drawing and painting.

Seated philosopher amongst personifications and disciples
Façade of a sarcophagus, marble, around 270
/ Vatican Museum, Museo Gregoriano Profano

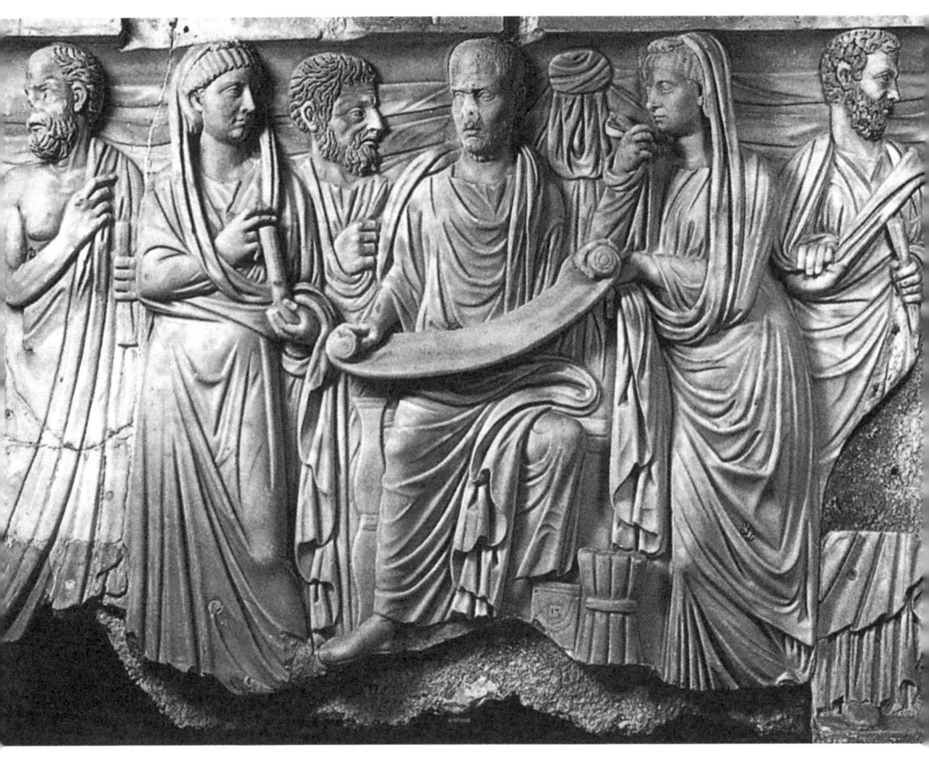

FIG. 12

Fragment of a relief of the Temple of Bel, in Palmyra, which portrays a religious procession – first century of our era. While this relief offers an excellent example of a complex scene brought to a single plane, the detail I reproduce here shows a group of veiled women which foreshadows, it seems, the characters of Romanesque sculpture. The two preserved figures reproduce the same rhythmical movement reflected by their silhouettes and the folds of their veil. These, without doubt, displace the real pattern of a fabric thrown on the head and shoulders by long parallel curves of almost geometrical regularity. Plastic research is absent, the folds only being engraved on a more or less planar surface.

Group of veiled women
Detail of a sculpted relief showing a procession, marble, first century AD, Temple of Bel, Palmyra / Palmyra, Syria, destroyed in 2015

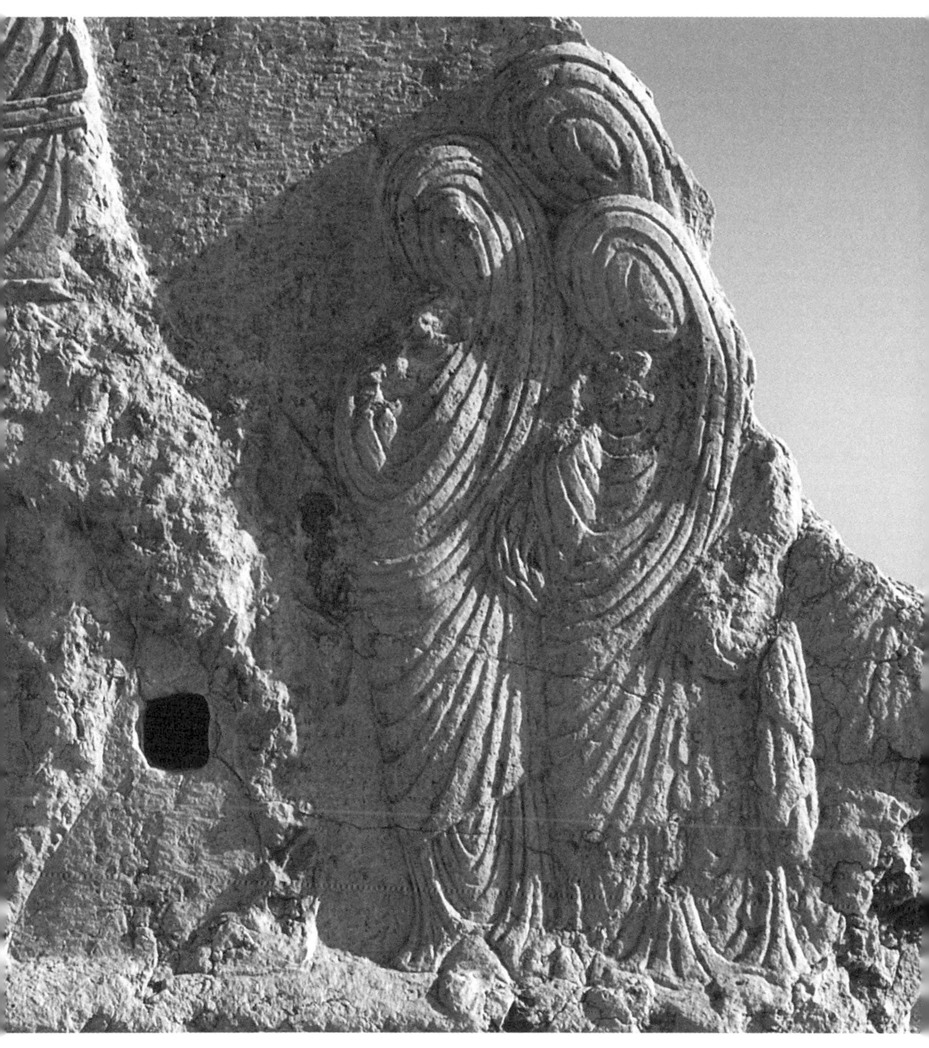

FIG. 13

Fragment of a fresco in the temple of Palmyrene Gods in Dura on the Euphrates. – Two priests and a high priest. Second century AD. Composition on a single and abstract plane, in which the painter simultaneously represents a rear wall and aligned figures which are partly identical; all frontally orientated. Except for the faces, attempt at plasticity is absent: the figures break away as big patches of local tones surrounded by a black outline and crossed by a net of narrow lines which figure the folds. Deprived of volume, these characters are also deprived of weight: their feet do not rest on the ground.

Scene of sacrifice by three priests
Fresco, first century AD, Temple
of the Palmyrene Gods, Dura-Europos
/ Dura-Europos, Syria

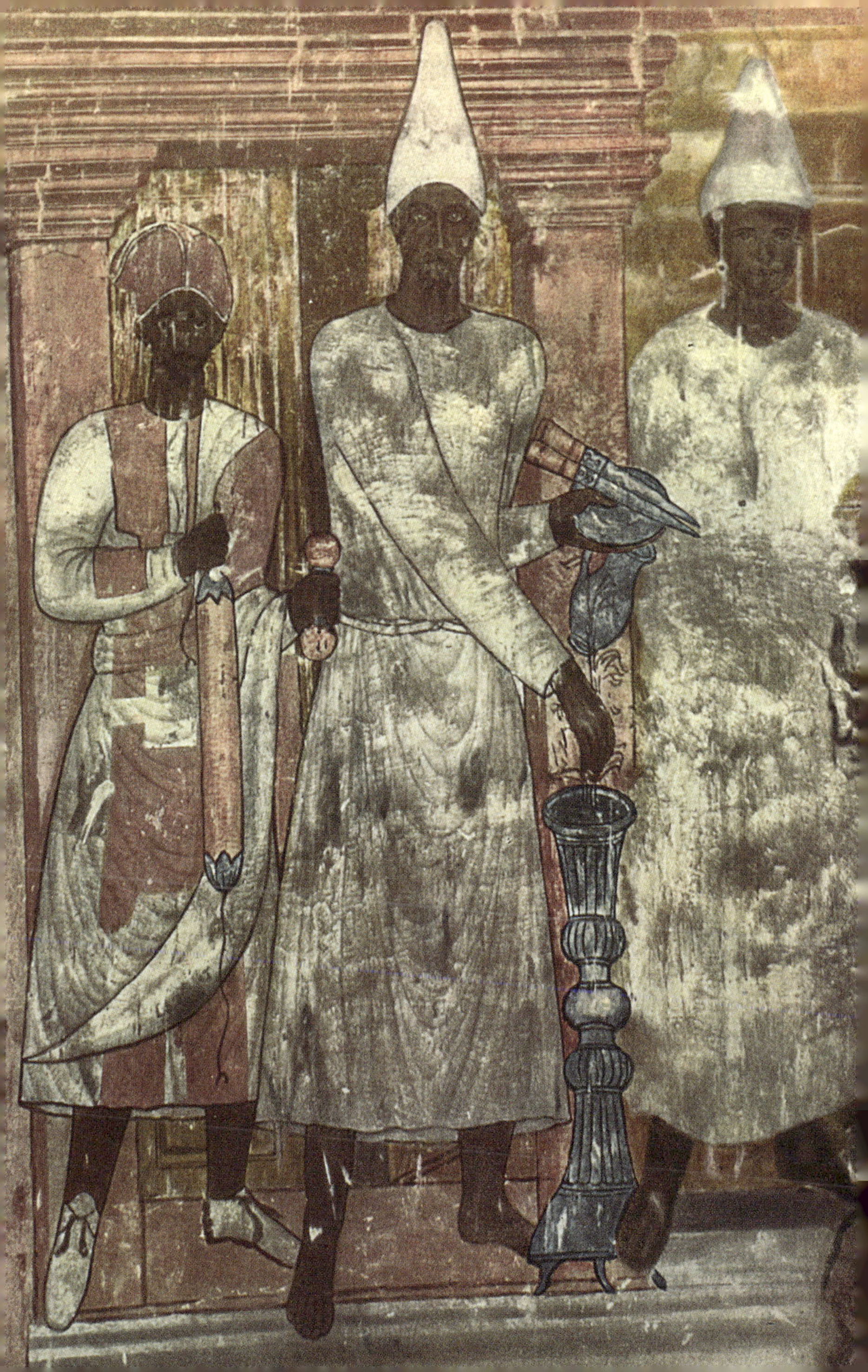

FIG. 14

Valve of the Symmachi-Nicomachi diptych. – End of the fourth century. Classical style.

"Symmachi Panel" of a diptych
Ivory, ca 400, Rome
/ Victoria & Albert Museum, London, Inv. № 212–1865

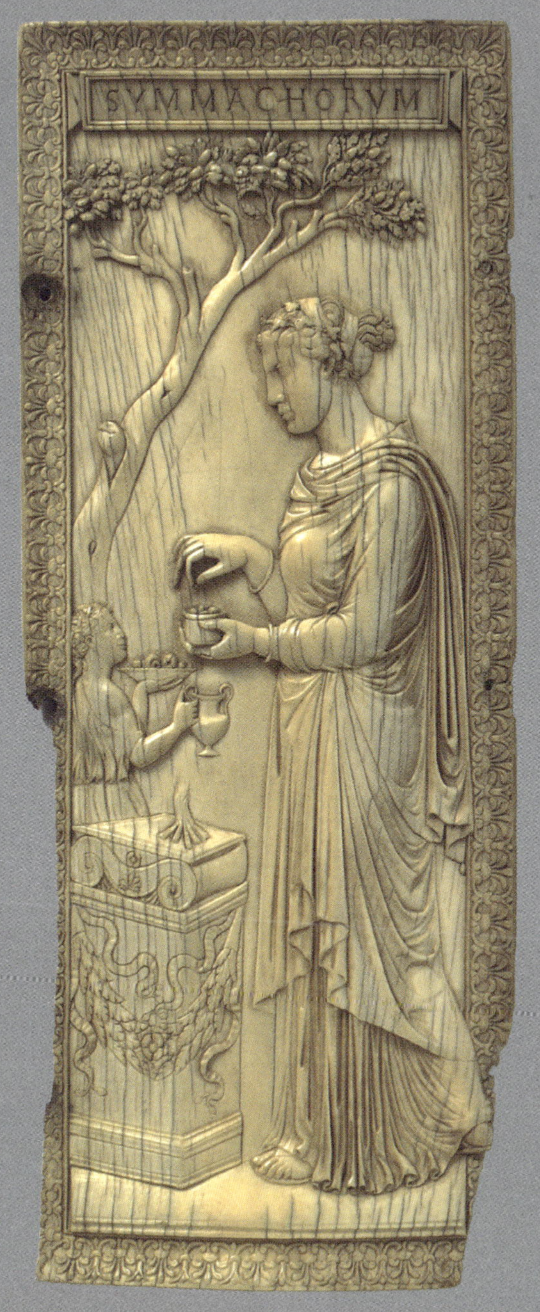
SYMMACHORVM

INDEX

INDEX OF PLACES

ANDRÉ GRABAR
PLOTINUS·AND·THE·ORIGINS·OF·MEDIEVAL·AESTHETICS

Printed by DIDOT, spol. s r.o. Trnkova 119, 628 00 Brno-Líšeň on the paper SENDme Laid Natural White 250 g/m² and IQ Print 120 g/m². Design and typesetting is done with use of the fonts Adobe Text Pro and Neftali Pro.

First edition, Brno–Roma 2018, 128 pages.
Number of copies: 500

info@earlymedievalstudies.com
info@viella.it

ILLUSTRATIONS

ILL. 1: from *Reden und Gedenkworte / Orden pour le Mérite für Wissenschaft und Künste*, XXIII (1990–1992), p. 59; ILL. 2: © Creative Commons; ILL. 3: © Archives Bourgogne-Gallé-Perdrizet; ILL. 4: from *L'Ecole Pratique des Hautes Etudes. Invention, erudition, innovation. De 1868 à nos jours*, Patrick Henriet ed. Paris 2018; ILLS 5–7, 9: scans from publications; ILL. 8: © State Historical Museum, Moscow, MS D.129; ILL. 10: © Tretyakov Gallery, Moscow; ILL. 11: © PNP, Fond Nikodim Pavlovič Kondakov, Fotografie, Studie, N. P. Kondakov s přáteli, № Přír: 165/42; ILLS 12, 13: scans from front pages of *Cahiers Archéologiques,* I (1945) and *Seminarium Kondakovianum*, I (1927); ILL. 14: from *La Syrie antique et médiévale illustrée*, René Dussaud, Paul Deschamps, Henri Seyrig eds, Paris 1931; ILLS 15, 16: scanned covers of André Grabar, *Le premier art chrétien*, Paris 1966 and *idem, L'âge d'or de Justinien*, Paris 1966 © Gallimard.

FIGURES

FIG. 1: from André Grabar, Carl Nordenfalk, *Le Haut Moyen Âge: du quatrième au onzième siècle*, Geneva 1957, p. 37; FIG. 2: © Biblioteca Apostolica Vaticana, Vatican, Vat. Gr. 0699, FOL. 63V; FIGS 3 & 6: © Creative Commons; FIG. 4: © KHM-Museumsverband; FIGS 5, 8, 9: photo author; FIG. 7: © Musée des Beaux-Arts de Dijon/ François Jay; FIG. 10: from Richard Delbrueck, *Antike Porphyrwerke*, Berlin/Leipzig 1932, PL. 50; FIG. 11: © Vatican Museums, Museo Gregoriano Profano; FIG. 12: © Annette Rossi; FIG. 13: from Franz Cumont, *Fouilles de Doura-Europos (1922–1923)*, 2 vols, Paris 1926, vol. 2: Atlas, PL. XXXII; FIG. 14: from Paul Williamson, *Medieval Ivory Carvings. Early Christian to Romanesque*, London 2010, cat. no. 3, p. 34.

In the matter of copyright, every author is responsible for the illustrations published. In general, the series PARVA Convivia follows § 31 of the law № 121/2000 Coll. (Copyright Act), where in paragraph 1 c explicitly states: "Copyright shall not be infringed by whoever uses a published work in a lecture exclusively for scientific, teaching or other instructive or educational purposes; the name of the author, unless the work is an anonymous work, or the name of the person under whose name the work is being introduced in public must however always be indicated; the title of the work and source must also be indicated."

PHOTOGRAPHIC CREDITS